# In The Afterlife

A Chronicle Of Our Experiences On The "Other Side"

Direct First Person Accounts
By Individuals On The "Other Side"
Via A True Full Body
Open Deep Trance Channel

# APRIL CRAWFORD

*AMAZON Top 50 Best Selling Author*

Title: **In The AfterLife:**
*A Chronicle Of Our Experiences On The "Other 'Side"*

Author: April Crawford

Publisher: Connecting Wave
2629 Foothill Blvd.
Unit # 353
La Crescenta, CA  91214
www.ConnectingWave.com

ISBN:  978-0-9823269-9-2

For Author Information:  www.AprilCrawford.com

Other books via April Crawford:
www.AprilCrawfordBooks.com

Book Design:  Allen Crawford

Cover and Appendix Review:  Dee Crawford
www.DeeCrawfordStudios.com

For Permissions:  Publisher@ConnectingWave.com

# Introduction

This book has been written by literally dozens of different individual authors, all of whom wrote their messages themselves personally and directly in letter or diary entry form via a true full body open deep trance channel and spirit medium. And, all of whom wrote their messages not just *about* the afterlife, but *from* the afterlife.

The string of adjectives in the description of the channel as a "true", "full body", "open", "deep", "trance" channel, all have a specific meaning within this field of work, particularly for this book, given the way it was written and by the many individual authors. The meaning of each adjective is explained in the Appendix to this book.

Here is the basic information about this collection of messages from those actually in the afterlife:

1) Each message was written by a different individual (except for Arthur, who wrote several).

2) Each message was written in first, final, and only draft. Not a single word has been changed. However, note that some punctuation was added, particularly apostrophes especially for contractions such as the word "I've", and commas. Also, a very few small words such as "a", "is" and "the" were added to make some short thoughts complete sentences.

Note that in most cases, the word "Me" was added to the end of the entry as a literary convention. For the first few letters, they did sign using "Me", even though all of the messages were written by different individuals (again, with the exception of Arthur). However, they soon stopped signing the messages with "Me" and I thought of not including a "Me" in any of the following letters. However, when the messages were being formatted for book printing, I realized that the "Me" at the end of each message had a subconscious effect that signaled the end of the message that seemed to make the reading more fluid. So, I made the executive decision to include a "Me" at the end of any message where a different signature was not used.

3) None of these messages were "relayed" to a medium who then wrote them down, nor were they written via what many people would term "automatic writing". Instead, each message was physically written directly by the author *via* the full body deep trance channel. In other words, April Crawford has the extraordinary natural (i.e., not learned) ability to go completely out, so that those nonphysical visitors, in this case individuals on the "other side", can come completely in. Thus, zero distortion. Zero "coloring" by the personality of the channel.

4) While some readers may wonder how it is possible to have such detailed messages from so many individuals communicating via any medium or channel, I can tell you that this level of communication is hardly as impressive as and amazing as the conversations that I and April's clients routinely experience during real-time sessions.

The reason is that our live sessions do not have the inherent limitations of what you can read in a book. The live conversations are fully two-way interactive and just as individual in nature as any conversation. And they *are* conversations in every sense of the word. They are not just one-way monologues by the visiting entity or individual in the afterlife. They can be quite casual, quite lively, and quite specific. For those of you who may have seen the YouTube videos of the entity VERONICA speaking, or if you have consulted directly with VERONICA yourself, either in person or by phone, you know what I mean. But also know that there are many others in addition to VERONICA who can and do speak (and write, and type).

Now, I do not wish to imply that the messages in this book were not done "live" and in real-time. They were. Many of those involved could if they wished, have spoken with me, used body language, and even gotten up from the table they were writing at and walked around the room. However, the focus of this project was for them to write their messages and not to have a social visit. Note that some did have other private visits with me where we had conversations, they got to look around the room, discover some of our pets, and even if they wished, have a sip of wine. Just as if they were fully present in the body of the channel. Because they were.

5) This book is not just a sequel to April Crawford's first book written from the afterlife, *"Parting Notes": A*

*Connection With The Afterlife.* *"Parting Notes"* was written by individuals about the moments just prior to, during, and just after their physical "deaths".

This book, *In The AfterLife,* on the other hand, has been written by individuals who are much more experienced in the afterlife. These are individuals who have learned how it works over there.

I would use this analogy. If *"Parting Notes"* were to be described as accounts from freshmen about getting on the bus for their first day at college and about their first day in the dorm room and their first day at class, *In The AfterLife* has been written by second term seniors, with a few graduate students and perhaps a professor in the mix.

In other words, those who wrote their messages from the afterlife for this book, know the ropes so to speak. They are not the wide eyed freshmen, but rather the much more experienced and substantially more mature individuals who have been around the block a few times.

6)  Some of the authors were motivated to write to a specific person that they had in mind.  These letters were included because they convey a great deal of information about being in the afterlife, even though they were written to a specific individual, who may or may not get to read them.

7)  It is important to note that although many people around the world have telephone and in-person consultations with the highly evolved entity VERONICA, April Crawford does not offer the services of contacting friends and loved ones after they have crossed over to telephone clients.  So please don't call after reading this book and ask for that.

While April is fully capable of this, there are many variables having to do with specific individuals, such as where they are focused at any given moment, how experienced they are on the other side, their level of interest in communicating, etc.

Accordingly, April only offers this type of communication with specific individuals who have crossed over as part of certain research partner investment programs intended to record and share what is learned with the world at large. Any client requesting such contact by phone with friends or relatives who are on the other side is referred by us to one of two professional relay mediums that we know, and who work in a manner similar to the well known psychics and mediums John Edward and James Van Praagh, who I mention only as examples that many people can relate to.

Hopefully, the above will go a long way towards illustrating what a true full body open deep trance channel is capable of. Note that especially with regard to the "*open deep trance*" part, these are very rare in the world at any given time, or for that matter, in history.

The above information is basically what I would like you to know about this book and how it was written. For some additional details (after you have read the messages) and a few related true stories about my life married to a full body open deep trance channel, check out the Appendix to this book.

-Allen, Facilitator for April Crawford

*"My mother crossed over a few years ago.  Had I not known what I have learned through this writing experience, I would have despaired.*

*I have proof within that she is fine and that I definitely will see her again."*

**-April**

*"Nothing is ever lost or wasted.*

*You <u>will</u> remember it all, and it will be forever."*

**-VERONICA**

*~ In The AfterLife ~*

Each of the following messages was actually physically written in first person directly by a different (except for Arthur) experienced individual (i.e. not a "newbie") who was currently resides, except during these extraordinary visits, on the "other side". This was possible because they were written via a true full body open deep trance channel and spirit medium.

These messages were not "relayed" to a medium who then wrote them down, nor were they written by what some people may think of as "automatic writing".

## ~ MESSAGE NUMBER 1 ~

October 11

I expected to live long. It was foretold to me in all the readings that I had aspired to in my youth. Nary a word was said of an early demise. So why was the moment snatched from my eager hands whilst I slumbered in the dark?

No one knew of my heart, least of all me. I was the banner of health for all to see. At least that was my belief.

So it was with great surprise that the hand of death gripped my heart that October morning. I felt the chill of the frost upon my bed sheets. My toes reached outward from the warm blanket whilst searching to awaken. I felt the remnants of a colorful dream dissipating softly from my thoughts.

The day as I knew it began to unfold in an array of color. Glancing at the clock, I realized with delight that there were exactly eleven minutes left before the burst of the alarm would summon me.  Slipping down to nestle under the warm comforter, I stole the extra moments with glee.

One intake of breath stopped all the thoughts of comfort as I struggled to take another but could not.  I wondered not what was wrong but thought only of my mother a hundred miles away who I now know would not hear from me today.

I expected more theatrics I suppose.  It was all rather short & sweet.  No time for the panic one would anticipate.

A grip so tight that I felt the covers move off the bed.  There I was exposed to the cool air but no longer really caring about the warmth.

I knew of course, but belief was slow in arriving.  The confusion being that there was not much difference in the experience.  Perhaps the most poignant was looking at the self I used to be.  The body inert and lifeless, whilst I still thrived while observing it.

My thoughts turned to my mother. Too old I knew to handle the twist in this drama. She would be distressed at the order, feeling of course that it should be her.

I struggled with the transition only whilst worrying for her. Interestingly, the scene before me blended into her home in a blink of an eye.

Marveling at the ability to move so fluidly, I waited at the edge of her bed to give her the news. Her eyes fluttered open and I marveled at how well she looked for seventy eight. She was thirty or more years older than I and in much better shape obviously.

I spoke softly to her relating the events, hoping somehow she would hear me and understand. I wished fervently that she could be prepared, after all this would not be good news to her ears.

The phone rang and I knew.

Her eyes brimmed with tears as I held her hand. I knew that we would have to wait until she was ready to join me.

It was all for the good as I got to know part of my mother I never knew existed. She felt me. I know it.

The time was short until her joining me. We both walked together into the next moment. Pleased I was, and grateful for the additional time spent with such a wonderful woman.

We both now continue. Another experience, another life. This time I will be the last to leave but I know intimately that she will wait for me as I did her.

Me

## ~ *MESSAGE NUMBER 2* ~

November 27

Being here in what was called the afterlife has been much more than I ever figured.

Admittedly, I was expecting what I had been taught in bible school. Pearly gates guarded by angels with the good Lord sitting in judgment. It seems that was all rather a fairy tale made up to make us all feel like it was gonna be so different.

Well, not so fast, it's more like an experience without solid or time. Took quite a spell for me to get use to new ways. Fact is that's much more comfortable than physical life.

I recollect arriving with my expectations in hand. It didn't take too long to know that all of that wasn't how it really was. Nobody sitting on a jury. No one to bow down to. Just me and all the loved ones I ever knew, plus ones I had forgotten.

It was bitter sweet cause it took some adjusting, but when all of it settled I realized how important it was to make a decision. Of course mine was to remain available for my family.

I could watch over all their decisions while still on earth. It was real interesting to see how time worked. It moved faster for some than others.

I felt a huge relief for being still connected to them.

It took me by surprise when my wife Alice showed up and told me she had spent 11 years without me. I simply forgot about time while viewing her moments. If I focused it sure didn't seem that long? Well maybe for them but not for me.

Alice and I are waiting now as well. Watching and sending vibration to our children. Hope to meet up with them real soon.

It's interesting here.  I would not create it any differently.

Still get mixed up about time though.  It just doesn't make sense where I am now.

-Arthur

## ~ *MESSAGE NUMBER 3* ~

November 30


I heard you wonder about me as I moved my energy through the space. You worried for my well being during my transition. The love between us never wavered though at the beginning of the journey I was unsure.

Meeting those I knew, and those I did not, did assure me that all would be well. Throughout it all I endeavored mostly to rejoin you as much as possible. For once the review concluded and I was left to decide the next moment, my thoughts raced towards the physical environment. This was deeply embedded in hope to reach you to let all know I was well.

It was fascinating to view your life as it went forward. I had clear memory of all our special times.

I did not lament but rejoiced in all of the energy shared. I began to feel you calling me and of course it was a difficult moment to know how to respond so that you would hear me.

Given the choice to move forward, I declined. Not because I was not intrigued. I knew your thoughts would call for me, I guess. So I decided to wait until it was time to connect.

At first it was just a sensation but eventually the words of your unrest came clearly forward. I admit frustration at the denseness that seemed impossible to permeate, but I persevered.

Ultimately there was a brief moment where I noticed you paying attention to my moving my energy through the light in our kitchen. It was an endless effort to assure you of my presence. It was with great joy that I perceived that you finally "got it".

So I feel you and "see" most events unfold for you. Still haven't been able to send a spectacular letter of my presence but I'm working on it.

My heart smiles when I watch you bravely moving on without my physical.

I know how hard it must be for you.  I am able to see you when you have not the opportunity.  Know that I am working on that as well.

I will not go beyond this level without you.  Know I am here.

Love,

Me!

## ~ *MESSAGE NUMBER 4* ~

December 1

Upon arrival there was much angst towards the process that brought me here. It was premature, the ending of that particular life. So much left unattended, not to mention those dear that were seemingly left behind.

I admit it took me a while to reconcile this death, however, now it has settled within me.

A moment of thought as to the advancement came and went swiftly. The primary focus being reconnected to those not able to make the journey with me.

Frustration built up as the inability to do so literally escaped me. I could feel your energy, see your actions, but could do nothing correctly to reach you.

The sense of time escaped my grasp as the process continued. Your appearance remained the same so I assumed that it was not a huge amount of time that had passed. Amazing that I could no longer sense automatically its passing.

I suppose it would have been less frustrating to simply move towards the next opportunity. I thought of it often but was always interrupted by the memory of your green eyes as they gazed into mine. It simply was not an option to leave without you.

So I wait. Not sure what to expect but the feeling of your energy soothes me. There are others here but I wish to only embrace you. I do not feel lonely as the others do blend, but I wait for the embrace of your soul with mine.

I continue to extend myself and who knows, perhaps success is but a breath away. You are worth the wait. I know you are waiting to get here as well.

I love you.

Then. Now. Always.

Me

## ~ *MESSAGE NUMBER 5* ~

December 7

Dear Friend,

The most impressive thing of it is the calmness. I never thought it would be like this, not that I had any expectations.

All the hearsay about angels and clouds was not exactly correct. In bible school they did mention heaven but haven't seen pearly gates yet.

There is this feeling of comfort, like none of the little things are bothering me. When I still had a body everything was a problem. Not here.

At first I wondered what time it was. Found out that it really didn't matter. I was already where I was going and it did not appear that I missed anything.

Oh. And I can see you if I want to. Yep. Right there in front of me. Looks like you are doing all right. Yes. I think about you all the time too.

There are others who say I will know when you're coming. I hope so.

They also say that the so called time apart will vanish and we will just be together. Some say I've been here twenty years already. That was a shock but it made sense when I thought about it. Our kids do look older when I visit. I only see how well they turned out, don't think much about time.

If that's all true then it's been a long time for you. It must be hard. I will try to send you a sign. It can be tricky but I will give it a lot of focus.

I love you! Of course you already know that but it feels good to say it.

Hope you see this.

I am missing you but doing fine. Just waiting for you.

I will explore this place more when you get here.

I know you have a lot still to do so I won't keep ya, but I will keep you in my heart.

Me

## ~ *MESSAGE NUMBER 6* ~

December 10

Dear Friend,

The sky opens to meet me. Odd how that occurs when one truly looks. I spent many years gazing at the sky. Never did I realize the expansiveness of its existence. My error occurred when I tried to see with my eyes instead of my soul. Upon my death those spiritual eyes suddenly grasped the enormity of the universe.

Each breath taken after death placed me in a vortex of energy that far surpassed anything I knew. The vastness of what we call the cosmos out runs any pretext of words. I truly do not think there is adequate vocabulary to describe it.

There was a moment where I thought of declining this communication as the language is inadequate. However, the need for any communication supersedes the quality. Thus I wrote in this primitive tongue to you dear friend.

I realize how the arrogance creeps in, but alas it is true. My mind is now filled with many languages, all of which I spoke at one time or another.

If possible, move past that moment to the truths that I bring you. There is a level of existence that encompasses more than you can comprehend. Now that I have left my physical form I can embrace that existence and become one with it. In the physical we are preoccupied with physical needs. Sometimes those needs help us evolve, other times they serve as a distraction.

I now see the whole picture. We communicate to open your eyes. Spiritually or Physically to another way of living. And we desire to comfort any fears that you associate with the end of physical existence. It simply does not apply to the vastness of your soul. Our goal is to communicate this. There is no other purpose.

We give you our word as spiritual beings that we speak the truth. For as spiritual, the truth is all there is. No drama exists here.  It is petty and unworthy of the richness of this plane.

Close your eyes and visualize if you desire a place beyond any expectation.  If you can create it in your mind, multiply it by a thousand fold.  That is where you will be when the physical is shed and you become your true self.

**T**

*[Note - Unlike the others who wrote messages for this book, T is a highly evolved nonphysical entity with at least hundreds of aspects, many of which have incarnated physically, each with their own "past lives".  Also note that April has not read the book "Parting Notes", which was written more than ten years ago.  I mention this because in some areas, T's message for this book, although expanded, is word for word identical to what he wrote as his message for "Parting Notes".  It is an amazing demonstration of "his" memory, at a minimum.  Perhaps T feels that this message is important enough to be re-emphasized.  -Allen]*

## ~ *MESSAGE NUMBER 7* ~

December 14

The silence envelopes me like a warm blanket on a chilly day. I remember such moments with you. At times they felt receded unto my thoughts so deeply it was difficult to recall exactly where they existed.

A continuous thread of memory sews a pattern revealing my lives as they unfold. I always thought they follow each other, picking up momentum as I approached the Promised Land.

Remarkably the Promised Land turned out to be my existence. Here and now I feel ever guided towards something magnificent. Even knowing all of the experiences, I realize I am still not finished.

We used to jest that we would wait for the other at heaven's gate. That was when we believed in a fabled here after. The real one is much more interesting, as it emphasizes continuance rather than an ending. Eternal is true but the journey towards it very different than what we thought.

Time used to be something I gave a great deal of thought to. Now I do not consider it at all. I know you count the days since I left as well as the ones to your arrival here.

I suppose I am the more fortunate one as I can see you continuously if I want to. And yes I still want to above all else.

If you think of it, reach out for me while you live your day. I believe I can help ease the difficulties. It would be worth a try.

It's all much better than we could have guessed. Know that I'm very close and the horizon is within my abilities.

I love you and await you. There is so much to share and instead of so little time, there is none at all. That way we just ignore it and lie endlessly embracing our love.

Me

## ~ *MESSAGE NUMBER 8* ~

December 21

My first thoughts were confused.  Where was I?

As I calmed myself, I began to understand that my physical death had occurred.  It wasn't a fear that enveloped me but a great disappointment of losing you.

With my guides I moved through a steady moment.  It was here that I began to understand what could be available if I tried.

And try I did.

Each breath of the body takes a bit of eternal space. Within those guidelines, I began to move closer to your energy.  It meant that each day in the way I remembered it was not available, but a connection with your energy was.

It did not take long to figure out what I wanted. Guides came forward with understanding and assisted me.

All I wanted was to see you, feel you, smell you. At first all I got was a static energy that in no way resembled you.

However, I persevered. I kept working on the vibration until I connected.

It is my belief that you felt it the first time I was able to pull it off.

It was a joyous occasion for me. The look in your eyes so clear. I knew that you felt me.

Now I wait.

I know you will join me soon. The wait a long one for you, however, the presence of you in my energy very comfortable.

There are other experiences, other opportunities, but what of them... without you?

Grateful for the ability to be in your energy. Knowing we will touch again, leaves me giddy with anticipation.

Touching your soul is good, but your hand in mine is worth the wait.

Me

## ~ *MESSAGE NUMBER 9* ~

December 22

I never felt this moment while I was still physical. Never considered my existence after death. Always thought you had your shot and then it was over. Done. Kaput.

Wishing sometimes to be able to see my mom again. Considered briefly the "what if" of an afterlife. Never though did I realize or consider how vivid and complex it actually is.

I use the present tense purposefully because my focus is exactly there. Considering before and after has become irrelevant. As much as I would like to shift my focus, I cannot. The present in the afterlife is all I can muster at the moment.

The first of it was different. I suppose my expectations were out of line with the real truth. But, what would you expect from a Catholic Mama's boy, eh?

The abruptness of my arrival gave no opportunity for preparation. Bam! "Here it is. You're now dead."

But I wasn't, at least my sense of self wasn't. It was difficult to accept but the alternative was not great.

So....

Here I am. There have been interesting moments for sure, but, all in all, not so bad.

I feel like a kid at camp, writing to his parents about his experiences. They being so much more than written, and the parents not really comprehending what goes on, really, at camp.

Sometimes I laugh to myself while the reality unfolds. I wish I could really relate the process, but I guess I can't.

I'm told it's all individual.

The perception of a loved one fills me and I understand what the purpose was in my life.

I guess the process of this is created by me.  I always had to do one thing at a time.  Happily I persevere, knowing there is no judgment.

Just thought you'd want to know I'm OK.

Me

## ~ MESSAGE NUMBER 10 ~

January 3

Love

Upon first glance, the afterlife appeared to be simple. A feeling of completeness enveloped what I now knew as me. Odd, since my life preceding was successful and fulfilling, or so I thought while living it.

There was a vivid memory of many lifetimes that at first felt very confusing. I never thought it possible to know all of them at the same time, but I can.

The simple surroundings had one focus. One thing that I knew deeply had more importance than anything.

You.

I found that by looking into your energy the surrounding of my own increased. Each memory, each touch, produced more complexity in my afterlife.

I became enraptured with your energy. Probably more so than when we both were there. Was that possible?

I would not have known the answer before. However, now I would say an enthusiastic "yes"!

It wasn't a life or a moment, but your energy and the "love" I associated with it.

I realized as I opened up more to the love for you, more appeared around me.

Suddenly it was much more all due to the love. It is a great lesson. I remember my father saying that "You can't take it with you."

The one thing you can take is the love. It creates a simple but embracing experience here.

I wish I had realized that more while still there with you.

Perhaps I will focus only on the love from here on out. By the time you get here, maybe there will be more.  The love exceeds any expectation of the hereafter.

Me

## ~ *MESSAGE NUMBER 11* ~

January 10

The experience of love is not overwhelming. It is a perfect blend of the experiences of so many lives and the me that now acknowledges them all.

While still in the physical I used to wonder how it would be to have all that information at once. My poor linear brain would literally short circuit when I thought about it. So I simply kept ignoring all the signs of my multiple experiences. It was easier to adhere to the standard practice of the one shot theory. That is until it was time to depart.

I found that I really liked living. Wanting it all to continue, I fought bravely to keep my self in the form. The body, however, had other ideas and retired way before I was ready. There was a fearful moment during my exit that thought about the idea of finite. Would I simply go dark? Would there be angels?

Would my parents greet me with loving embraces?

All the thoughts distracted me as I was lifting out of that tired old body. (There was a good riddance moment or two as well.)

I was surprised to feel like me. All of my thoughts were suddenly enhanced with all of the memories of other experiences. Funny. I did not even consider all of the differences, only the similar energy of all of them.

Now, it takes much concentration to write in a line let alone live one. I chuckle with the memories. Apparently I've had quite a few interesting moments. Well worth the wait to engage them. So different but familiar as I've obviously been here before.

It's not the end. The body withers but your ideas, thoughts and experiences continue.

There is not doubt. I am right here in it all.

-Arthur.

## ~ *MESSAGE NUMBER 12* ~

January 11

Dear friend,

The suffering is not but a distant memory, that lingers briefly then fades away.

Leaving the body is more difficult than coming in is... at least in my experience.  Coming, the conditions are known while leaving the conditions in most cases are forgotten. Physical density has a way of clouding the perspective I suppose.

Being here is fulfilling.  There is more availability to connect than I knew.  That eased my angst quite a bit upon arrival.

All questions not immediately answered, but a comfort of continuance making up for it.

The rhythm of the body created a vibration that was not evident here. It took a moment to realize what was missing. The vibration of physical is often disregarded as one progresses through it. Being one of the first things I noticed, it seemed important to mention it.

Feeling the new effects of the current environment was of interest. I can capture all experience in a single thought. I'm talking about the multiplicity of life experience outside of the time line (which I perceive very vividly). They all blend but also remain separate.

I feel wonderful. The last moments extremely hard. Know that that no longer affects me.

What I do next is often upon me. There are other energies that present themselves, I suppose for counsel. Not having availed their assistance yet, I linger in the rapture of feeling good. A great gift though there is no body to display it.

Curious.

That is how I would sum this up. Know that I am still here. The word here being a variable (chuckling to myself).

Will write again when ready.

Me

## ~ *MESSAGE NUMBER 13* ~

January 10

I recall talking about crossing over and how once I made it to heaven I would be in touch.

Well, I made it here but it is quite a different scenario than I was given. The death not such a harrowing experience, a simple turn of the cheek. The arrival without incident. It was the settling of pre-beliefs that was the kicker.

I remember feeling a bit anxious for the heavenly surrounding. Not that it was in the brochure. I chuckle to myself as I write because I know most will cringe that the brochure is inaccurate. So be it... I feel but there are no fingers to touch.

I hear but it is not a heavenly choir. It is the hum of my vibration although there are a few profound artists here who make heavenly music.

I see but it is not the imperfect moments of the physical. It is the love embracing all who perceive (and even those who don't) the collective energy.

If I were to give it a close comparison in the physical, I would say that it is like an electrically charged embrace. It is mellow, even for the most abrasive types. I know, because I have seen it.

Taste is irrelevant because there is nothing that needs to be eaten. If I dream I can taste whatever it is I miss, but there is no need for food.

I can smell the aroma of an open fire burning fall leaves if I so desire. It is more of a vivid memory come to life, but equally satisfying.

I touch but it is not with physical hands. It's a hard decision, which is more endearing... a physical hug or spiritual one. I like 'em both to tell you the truth.

Settling here is easy after you lose the expectations. No disappointment, only clarifications. I feel at peace. I feel warm in the embrace of all who love me.

Couldn't be better.

Well, maybe could be if you were here to share it.

Me

## ~ *MESSAGE NUMBER 14* ~

January 1

Being dead is not as macabre as it sounds. I've never felt more alive truth be told.

The opportunity to reflect on experiences of all my participations has been and is enthralling.

There is ability to view the dramas, the good and the bad. My emotions run high merely speaking of them. Yes. There are emotions. Yes. There are thoughts. Yes. There are connections to others here in this vastly interesting place commonly referred to as heaven.

It isn't like the standard definition though. It's more like additional opportunity to learn and grow from a different view point. Awareness of where I have just come from is totally available. There was so much joy within knowing I could still participate with my family, albeit from a different vibration.

The body is a different memory at the moment since there is no immediate interest to return to another, at least for now.

I feel my loved ones so vividly. Each of their souls beyond what I expected. Seeing all of our connections solidifying my beliefs of our vast closeness.

There are no physical infirmities, I suppose because I am not "in" at the moment. A silly statement I realize, however, I have to keep reminding myself that I am in the afterlife. The experience is so colorful, it's easy to forget.

Know that I am better than fine. I see and feel it all. I hope you feel me even though you most likely cannot see me. (Not from a lack of trying, mind you.)

See you soon.

Dad

## ~ *MESSAGE NUMBER 15* ~

January 13

I was always afraid to die.

There were so many fables and opinions on what happened that it left me bewildered and confused. As it approached I fought tooth and nail to cheat death. Resorting to absurd treatments, hoping for a reprieve from what would come over take me.

In the last moments, I admit I was a bit juvenile in my grip upon life. Clutching anything I could, my tears were witnessed by those who loved me but could do nothing to stop the process in place.

Upon arriving, I again admit my inability to process information correctly. The scenario was one of tranquility and support disrupted by my hysterical assessment of a situation I thought to be tenuous at best.

Of course I was immediately calmed by something so serene that I stopped mid-hysteria to marvel at how well I suddenly felt.

A bit of embarrassment followed by extreme relief that I continued, left me speechless (perhaps for the first time) at what was unfolding.

Pockets of energy brought forth faces that I recognized. Each smiling with welcome as I calmed a little more.

Feelings of connection that had never really reached me while in life suddenly revealed themselves.

Overjoyed, I reached towards them, realizing how much I'd missed them. It was surprising how much I now remembered even though it was not from the immediate preceding life.

I had vaguely considered reincarnation but eventually dismissed it while becoming engaged in some religious dogma.

Yet here it was a love so deep that it was incredible to me that I had never thought of it till this moment.

I think I understand thoroughly the need to forget and move on to another life though. I never would have had the experiences in this immediate past life if I had remembered all the love and details of the one before that.

So confusing but now so simple. I race towards them gleefully knowing there is much to catch up with. Did they have experiences as well?

The one true thing here is that my fear of death was unfounded.

It is truly the beginning of the next phase. I guess I always figured it was the end.

Boy, was I wrong.

There is so much more.

-Me

## ~ *MESSAGE NUMBER 16* ~

January 17

Getting here was not exactly the simplest of things. Living was pretty important to me. My family was my first thought while moving out of my body. I would have wanted it different but it was what it was.

I could see all of them while wanting to console them. If I could have sent a message of any sort, I would have. The question is, would they have been aware enough to notice? I still do not know for sure.

So making it a quest, I started interacting as much as I could. Nothing seemed to work and I admit it was pretty frustrating. The odd thing was that I began to notice other things around me.

At first I did not feel any sort of presence, but I was so focused on my family I didn't care. After some time though, I could feel others. The surrounding shifted a bit until the outlines became visible.

Soon there were what looked like people surrounding me. Frankly it annoyed me because it was distracting me from my family.

I knew, though, eventually I would have to face them so I turned and engaged them.

It turns out they were guides who helped me attain a better perspective. With a laugh I asked where St. Peter was. They informed me that it did not appear as part of my belief system so I did not create it.

That shut me up for sure.

I had to think about that for awhile.

Soon I realized I could create anything if I wanted. So, I said "I want to go back."

They all replied that I could but then it would be somewhat impossible to connect with my family.

So I opted to stay but reside in the energy deeply. This allows total contact with physical if that's what I want.

And I do.

It's the best of both worlds I guess.

Me

## ~ *MESSAGE NUMBER 17* ~

January 18

A crowd surrounds me as I attempt to gather myself.  At first it felt as if nothing would ever balance itself out.  There were voices speaking in muffled tones as I strained to hear them more clearly.

I was surprised to find so many near when clearly I had just been alone.  It took quite a bit of ponderance to conclude that I had crossed over.

No one most likely noticed, with my biggest worry being my cat Oscar who would be dismayed not to be fed in a timely fashion in the morning.

Of course knowing Oscar, I witnessed his break in of the cupboard.  He munched greedily after ripping the neatly closed food bag I had left on the shelf.

Well I was glad for it.  A neighbor took him in after they found me tucked under my coverlet that January morning. Good for you Oscar.

I've since identified the hum of voices that greeted me. Some were from other times and places, while others obviously more experienced than I traded energy with me.  I surmised that they were guides.

I did not have immediate family to hover over, being that I was a bit of a loner in my life.

It turns out that most of those of whom I shared intimacy were from other lives.

You know, I always wondered about that past life stuff. Turns out it's true.  And I view a life where I was beheaded... guess that explained the neck pain that no doctor could find real evidence of.

I chuckle to myself how a lot of life's mysteries are all explained so easily here.  Think I'll stay here awhile.  It's fairly intriguing.

Much more so than physical.

Yes much more.

Maybe Oscar will show up.  Now that would be fine.

Me

## ~ *MESSAGE NUMBER 18* ~

January 24

I have to say getting here was much harder than being here. So much for the journey being the best part.

Obviously there is a bit of a chuckle under my breath as I make these statements.

My deaths, and yes I am making that plural, always seem so dramatic and over the top. Why not a simple go to sleep? Seems there's always drama afoot when it's time for me to return to spirit. Won't bore you with all those details, since what I want to tell you is about now.

Can't' tell you how long I've been here. Haven't thought about time in a while. See, there I go. It's hard to write a letter and not slip into time mode of some sort.

Long story short.

I am here in a continuing experience of bliss.  Yes, I said bliss.  There's a feeling of being connected to this larger energy that leaves me wondering why anyone would leave here in the first place.

I would say it's fluid in texture.  A feeling of knowing all these people and knowing that they are all you.  Really set me thinking.

I can expand myself to be where I want even if it's where you are in the physical.  That part's pretty hard but I've gotten better.  Nope.  Thinkin' I'll stay here for a spell.  Much better.  Happy.  Content.  Here.

Me

## ~ *MESSAGE NUMBER 19* ~

January 25

When I was alive physically I was always fascinated by electricity. Spent many an hour making primitive conduits to see where it would go. If there be a storm, I chased the thunder and black clouds, hoping to be struck. Of course, I never made the connection.

I more'n likely would have been electrocuted before my twelfth birthday.

There wasn't much special about me so when I did die, I was fairly surprised at what I found.

There be so much energy that at first it reminded me of an electrical storm of my childhood. At first I couldn't see much, but the electric pulsation continued to increase until I had like a movie going on in my head. Pictures of places I had been were starting to come fast.

Up till then I did not see much. I wasn't a church going fella so I did not expect angels or anything.

Once the electric storm began there was something there. I did know it was good. Maybe God or the like.

Once again I was fascinated with electricity. This time though, I could be part of it.

Maybe I'll be reborn so I can take some of the stuff I know back with me.

The electricity takes shape and I see my mom. Boy she looks darn good. She's wavin' me on. Suppose I should go see what she wants.

Sure do like this place. It's like I came from here.

Oh, and there's Mi Maw!

Sorry, I have to get going.

Me

## ~ *MESSAGE NUMBER 20* ~

January 26

There are parts of being in the world that I do not miss. The finite parts where becoming part of a timeline that results in deterioration. I guess that would be the part I miss the least.

Being on what is called the "other side" is free. That is the best word I can use. Free.

There are moments where I can clearly feel like I am still in a body. One that is at its optimum level. Not the aged or damaged level. It's interesting to feel that way again but I would not trade this existence for anything.

I always worried I would lose my individuality. That somehow I would be mixed in a huge vat of all my other experiences until the "I" would become a "we". Well, it is a "we", but, I am still the "I". An interesting contrast to all the stories I heard in my former life. It just isn't so.

It's like all the thoughts in your head are there but if you so desire, one thought can be brought forward and enjoyed.

Do not worry about loss. There is nothing but gain as far as I can see. All the memories of the other lives are part of me. And of course, I am part of them. It's not a separation, but a blend.

You will remember it all. I do.

If you are wondering about the "why" of it all, perhaps amend that to "why not?"

Nothing here is out of reach. No decline, only elevation. I may go back to the world again as more experience is good. If I end up here, all the better.

It is great.

Me

## ~ *MESSAGE NUMBER 21* ~

January 27

I spent a good part of my last life in search of the spot I currently reside in.

Yes. I am dead, technically speaking. However, there has never been a more alive feeling within me.

Being physical, especially this last go around, was not easy. Something never felt right. Even as a child I was always walking a narrow ledge. Never was there a comfort for being there, I was always out seeking another perspective.

Yea, I was pretty much a drug addict. Though it was looked at as escape, it was really me looking for this place all along.

The physical world is a hodgepodge of difficulty. It's so hard to maneuver through! I missed the serene feeling of the afterlife and was hell bent on gettin' back to it.

No matter how hard I tried I could never manage to jump the space.

Finally in the end, it was my heart that gave out.

So be it.

I was ready.

Now the feeling is that of content. If I can avoid it, never will I return to a physical environment. From what I understand, it is my choice.

So I choose here.

The flow around me is pristine.

I can create whatever I desire. Why would anyone or thing leave here?

It is a tapestry of thought.

My thought.

My universe.

My home.

So be it.

Me

## ~ *MESSAGE NUMBER 22* ~

January 31

Each time I arrive here it becomes more expansive. At first I need to settle down, so rigorous the journey is... at least for me.

It is true that one remembers it all. I did not believe that the first couple of go-arounds so it didn't happen. Looking at it now, it would have been different if I had just focused.

There was always a rush to return that did not allow for considering the whole process. In retrospect, I wonder what the hurry was all about. Did I feel urgency to continue something? Must have.

Now that I am more experienced there is ability to appreciate the surroundings. Maybe that's what evolution is... realizing and appreciating fully your surroundings.

Somehow I feel better this time. I am aware of others that did not seem to be here before. Perhaps I linger a while to get what this is all about.

No rush to return just yet. The parameters are expanding as I write. The focus necessary to do this is receding.

Yes, it is magnificent.

Hard to focus, dually.

When I decide to incarnate again I will relate my findings.

Adieu.

-Francis

## ~ *MESSAGE NUMBER 23* ~

February 1

I admit I did not appreciate the "living" much while I was there. It all seemed so contrived and trivial that I did not feel any true connection to it.

Most of it was spent misbehaving I guess. However, some of it had value but not enough to keep me there.

My passing in a dramatic was inevitable. When you do not value something it is easily taken from you. So passing was a slippery slope into what I figured was oblivion. At least that's what I hoped.

It did not turn out so well, this search for oblivion not really an option in the so called big picture. Finding myself yet in another environment was a bit of shock to say the least.

There was no one judging the event called my life. That did surprise me a little. So much for all the bible stories.

What was very vivid was all of these other experiences. The not so past lives as I like to call them. Little bits of information that all go together to give you a complete synopsis of you. I have to say though surprising, it was very intriguing.

So what now?

Well, it's more than just a participation in an event. It's a complete package, so to speak.

Still processing my inability to get the message of this most previous life. I suppose that could be rather lengthy. Anyway, here I am, or should I say, here we are. Probably more accurate.

Whoever designed this process was pure genius, or at least able to be all things at once. An experience I am having now. Interesting.

The return to the body awaits me, hnowever, there is still more to process... and I am.

Next time more appreciation.

This is quite a unique design, one that should not be taken for granted.

-Me

## ~ *MESSAGE NUMBER 24* ~

February 4

When I was embodied I always looked to the heavens for solace. The expansiveness of space appealed to me more than the limited earth environment.

I use to watch everyone scurry from point to point, always mindful of the time. It all exhausted me to a level of detachment that most did not understand.

Walking through the physical life was not easy for me. There was always an urgency to complete and get on with it. I suppose I always desired to go home to an environment of peace and tranquility. Obviously physical life did not offer that to me.

So after much dramatics I left the physical. Once completed there was such a relief of pressure. It was if my material state was truly an eternal one.

Of course all the belief systems of linear could have come into play, but since I didn't have any solid ones, I arrived peacefully.

It was such a pleasant moment, no theatrics, just a feeling of being home.

Anything that needs to be, one can be if one focuses creatively. If I desire connection, there is opportunity. If I do not then solitude is available. There is no sense of loss. If I wish to create a somewhat physical drama I can. Of course since it was not my particular preference, I do not.

I realize that incarnating into physical is a choice. The access to all of those experiences is rather available somewhat like a reference library in my thoughts.

I write purely for those who are like me. Those who do not find physical all that fulfilling. Knowing that there is a choice would have been a great comfort to me while traversing through a difficult life.

I now prefer to stay here.  Here being an extremely relative term, I suppose.

I choose to continue my expansion more on a more refined dimensional level.

Just thought it might be of interest.

Me

## ~ MESSAGE NUMBER 25 ~

February 5

I've decided to remain in this cocoon of comfort forever. There is no longer the insistent energy to move myself into another physical experience. The feeling of completeness overwhelms me as I connect with others of the same origin.

Wondering always about this experience, many beliefs and ideas were presented. Most I disregarded out of hand, but one always gave me pause.

It was the idea of a heaven. A condition described with angels and clouds that totally grabbed my attention as a child. I carried a secret hope that it would be as described. A totally loving place where all those you had lost would be waiting with open arms for your arrival. A great party from which one would never leave for eternity.

So I admit, upon my death, a small yearning for just that moment. A small gift for a life filled with disturbance and difficulty.

Well it turned out to be much better than that. No it wasn't a fairy tale filled with dreams and promises. It is an actual state of being that supersedes all expectation.

So there was no disappointment, only amazement. Yes everyone of importance was there and then some.

The only difference was my ability to keep creation within my grasp. So many more opportunities. The best part is the security created by all the love. Truly a cocoon environment to continue to evolve. I can create any way I want.

Yes I am staying right here with all of this warmth. Better than any physical life I ever had (and I now realize I've had quite a few).

Me

## ~ *MESSAGE NUMBER 26* ~

February 6

I was scared at first. The vehicle I participated in gave out and was no more.

One never looks at death as a bridge. The usual perception is that once the body goes all bets are off. "Every man for himself." "Get there any way you can."

All of it is pretty hilarious now, but in those moments, a frantic adventure. I suppose I fall into that frantic territory, even though I had heard all the alleged prophecies associated with death.

Funny. When death is upon you there is never the desire to go, but a great sense of "I wanna stay." At least that's the way it was for me.

I can look at the whole experience now with a sense of accomplishment. I did it! I made it through!

It wasn't nearly as arduous as I believed, but I am glad I exist here and now.

Here.

Where exactly is that?

That would have been my cheeky question in my younger moments. I am sure there are those who will read this wondering where in the heck I am.

Well, it's here. There is no solid moment. It is not measured in any way, shape, or form. One has to adjust to a multiple level theory of thought. Gone are the days of simplistic linear. However, I am not lamenting.

In energy form I am able to condense matter if I choose, or stay as a mist upon the ground. Whatever I decide, it is done.

The theory of energy and mass is relative but not how I go about my participation. A relief to be able to do what I think. A lot easier here than there.

Here is wherever my energy is. There is no sense of time or is there a sense of linear solid. However, I can perceive and participate along those lines if I desire.

I realize that this is not a scientific forum so I will forgo the speech about particles and string theories.

All that is important is the clearness now available with the absence of time and matter.

Does it matter?

Not to me.

Nor will it to you. This arena offers infinite puzzles and perceptions to explore. Why not?

Once you arrive you most likely will delay a return to physical. Except maybe as a recreational moment.

There should be no fear.

The energy is benevolent as you will be.

No icing of a heaven, pure creation opportunity.

Me

## ~ *MESSAGE NUMBER 27* ~

February 7

Throughout my existence there have been times of great distraction. Often in the physical environment, the feeling of isolation would leave me desperate to return. Where?

I did not know then. So confused was the experience, there would be no way of clarity for me.

The memory of worry that something important was missing kept me from knowing what to do. So it was with great relief that it ended. The concept of end though, is completely wrong... another difficulty for me since now the clear moments are always available.

In this eternal place of comfort the access is provocative in its vastness. There is an expanse of awareness that cannot be measured or would one want to do so.

I can feel all of my experiences. The value widely ranging in each one individually. Therefore, the sum of all being becomes the truth and not a snippet of consciousness.

Preferring this state, I remain. The moments most cherished being available to participate within.

Most I have known reside in the space within my energy. Among the beloved, a whole universe of experience awaits. Much preferred, much preferred.

I acknowledge the value of the physical, however, the freedom to be is more interesting.

Create experience. Create experience. It doesn't end, it just gets easier without the dramatics. There is no need for that now.

Me

## ~ *MESSAGE NUMBER 28* ~

February 8

All the talk of a heaven can be confusing while focused in the body. I recall the words that left me feeling unsatisfied with the perception of the afterlife. Why would it be a glorified version of the physical?

Certainly the lack of cohesiveness would bring about a more complex variable of the conscious mind. A sense of oneness and unity not the prevalent concepts in physical life. Well, at least it wasn't in my most previous experience.

I will admit a certain excitement knowing I was about to leave the body. Funny how attached one becomes to it while living. It simply is only a fraction of who I am. Now it's much easier to understand, especially without all the parameters.

What I appreciate most in the afterlife is the multiple awareness of experience. Feeling all my participations as they unfold is a great gift. The moments of fault and difficulty often overrun with accomplishment and growth. Much better to see it all instead of just a moment or two.

Personally I have had a few sour lives, that had I been defined solely by them, I would be upset.

So here we are in the oneness of all.

Platforms of definition are available if I should so choose to create them. All is fluid as I sit in a childhood tree house deciding which strand of energy to move into.

I delight in the vastness of it while I hold dear the special solid moments. It all is there. It is my energy. I am the creator. The oneness fills me and I am home.

Me

## ~ *MESSAGE NUMBER 29* ~

February 9

There is no sense of physicality.  My thoughts perceive one if I go in that direction, but that is not often.

I always wondered what it would be like to be here. Not the death process so much but the actual participation. Without a brain would I still be able to think?

As a matter of fact, I can.  However, the level of thought is more complex.

Memories are rather tiered in a multiple way so that I can process it all as a whole, or go to each individual experience.

While in a body that would be too difficult to do, or at least for myself it would be, not to mention all the other incarnated selves.

Never thought I would get to talk about this with anyone still physical. It certainly would not have been on my list of reading in the last life. I guess evolving can happen anywhere and for that I am appreciative.

Me

## ~ *MESSAGE NUMBER 30* ~

February 9

Coming of age as a soul.

I remember being here briefly on my determined march to the next experience. A blur of energy as I moved through the choices to the next life.

As I grew more experienced there was more awareness. A sense of oneness was comforting, but I retained the individuality that was very confusing at first.

Each time it became more clear though. This time, spending a greater amount of focus upon my energy. I suppose that means I will spend more "time" here. It does not feel that way. It's a struggle to focus upon time in this environment. Its endless parameters do not lend support to counting the moments. It's like a continuous idea that is not broken by interruptions.

It's difficult to use this form to create symbols that will translate into thought patterns. Not the most natural way to portray thoughts.

It's actually more productive here. I suppose there are many who decide to continue evolution from this perspective. Especially after a lot of growth.

Whatever I wish to experience, I can. Admittedly not as profound due to the density. So I can appreciate younger souls needing the density of the environment to finally "get it".

I now prefer this perspective.

More comprehensive.

More complete.

Linear reality is but one of the choices.

Me

## ~ *MESSAGE NUMBER 31* ~

February 10

For the moment there is a sensation of calm. A rest of sorts that is needed to the inner most part of my being.

Physical participation is a challenge compared to this. Still not sure of why there is such a process. Why not stay here in the warmth of the loving energy?

I do not really know what the surroundings would be defined as. There is not yet an opportunity to decipher the particulars. All I really know is the love. I feel familiar energies around me. It comforts me to realize their presence and their devotion. I do not feel alone, but there is no crowd.

A vibration translates to a thought as a picture of sorts unveils itself. Again I step into the love. The rest irrelevant in its rapture.

At times in my life, I supposed an arena of pearly gates so often described to me as a child. There are no gates, for structure of that kind does not thrive here. I do feel my family who have been here longer. I feel a sense of arms around my energy. They gently soothe me and I become peaceful.

There are words whispered of connection and continuance. I feel so complete. However, I laugh to myself that the completeness does not have solid structure. Perhaps though, it does. Perhaps the place of comfort and solitude is the essential epitome of soulfulness.

I am happy.

There is no need in this moment to venture forward to another experience. Not yet. This is such a sublime experience I wish to dawdle a while more.

I am blissful.

Me

## ~ *MESSAGE NUMBER 32* ~

February 14

There are many ways to evolve energy in all of the dimensions. Some souls have preference while others randomly seek their place in different processes.

We have talked to many who do not have an appreciation for the physical. Some of it is due to difficult dramas while others are at odds with the energy vibration.

The truth of the physical participation lies in the unique ability the physical offers to souls of all levels. It does take great boldness from a soul to move through all the denseness of the linear. If one can keep open to the energy, great evolution may be available to souls with the courage to walk through it.

Physical life was designed for evolution of the soul. Great strength is required. Know that all of you have the inner strength to boldly walk through any life. Even the creation of difficulty represents a soul with great boldness.

Perhaps reconsider the experience. Be proud of your boldness. Move through it all while in alignment with your energy.

It is indeed possible.

The rewards infinite.

You are brave enough to do it.

Me

## ~ *MESSAGE NUMBER 33* ~

February 15

I always worried about death. For those I loved, the idea of separation drove me to tears. The loss of connection was an event that I felt determined not to experience. Of course when a death did occur, I would spend countless hours in pursuit of their souls.

My death took me by surprise. The old heart simply gave out. No warning, no drama, no reprieve... done.

At first it took me a moment to regain my balance. Never liked surprises and this was a big one. So with great determination I set out to reconnect from this side. Actually, extremely interesting from a completely different point of view.

I still have a perception of my physical self. Often there is a difficult moment when I need to remind myself that I am considered "dead". Far from it.

This place, if one can really identify it as a place, is vast and fascinating. It's not just what has been described by religious perspectives. It is actually more of a space than a place. The parameters, if I wish to define them, are endless. In fact it is safe to say, there are none.

If I feel the need to retire to a heavenly moment, I of course can. However, it is far more exciting to break past all the perceived barriers into infinity.

I always reach as close to those I love as I can. Sometimes it is easier than others. Now I realize that all my efforts to connect while in physical were enhanced when the soul involved actually understood the process.

Glad to know I have advanced this far. There was always a worry or two about it while in the body.

Since nothing is measured here I suppose the infinity of my love for those still in the physical will transcend all barriers.

Perhaps after more experience, I can better articulate some helpful hints.

- Cedric

## ~ *MESSAGE NUMBER 34* ~

February 17

There was always a deep longing with me to know the non-physical. Most did not possess my curious nature on the subject. Most hoped their death was a far off event that did not need to be acknowledged, at least not immediately.

Some of my most endearing friends would shun it completely. That left me without an audience most of the time. The lack of cohesiveness that the experience provides gives one a unique perspective. My thoughts clearly recall the body but the immediate moment feels expansive. It takes a while for one's thoughts to adjust to consciousness without form... so programmed through habit this physical experience is. At first it was quite difficult to process the "me" without the me. Sounds ridiculous, doesn't it?

Forgive my flippancy but a grand experience it is.

The ability to take shape on command or expand the energy beyond perceived guidelines is fascinating.

It takes a great deal of practice until one can define all of the selves. That was one I was not ready for, all the selves. Past lives was not really part of my vocabulary, but it's all there. Fascinating.

The idea of energy within a great one-ness of thought really cannot be defined on this paper.

Know though, it is infinite. The possibilities endless. All of the data available with concentration, but I prefer no boundaries. It's better than I every dreamed it could be.

Me

## ~ *MESSAGE NUMBER 35* ~

February 22

I suppose the predominant experience here is the fact that I feel whole again.

This past incarnation was difficult. The end years were a series of declining moments. Each year bringing another loss of mobility until there was really nothing left to lose.

In those moments the laments from my heart were many. Endless suffering as the body declined. Hard pressed to recall any easy moments in those days.

A rush of enthusiasm greeted me upon my arrival here. Yes, here in this serene haven of bliss commonly called the hereafter. A great relief from the cumbersome biological body that no longer functioned with any clarity.

A rush of warmth enveloped my energy (which still felt somewhat biological). It gave me the notion that a lot of biology is really thought.

I digress.

This moment is blissful. The feeling of completeness is the main focus of this conversation. I feel whole. The lack is now [transformed to] abundant. The memory still exists but its enactment now is a memory.

The other lives take more center stage of the experience. They all co-mingle but can be drawn upon as singular if so desired.

I am whole.

Realizing your last memories of me are reflective of a diminished me. I reach towards you. No longer am I less.

We are never just the body. We are infinitely so much more. I now reside in the "more".

Worry not for me.

I am home.

Me

## ~ *MESSAGE NUMBER 36* ~

March 1

This thing called death is quite misrepresented. Whilst still breathing I recalled all of the legends of the experience, finding fault with most. For lack of clear answers, I put the question aside, never embracing it again until the moment of departure.

I felt the movement of my body no more as I allegedly slipped into the afterlife. I must admit that the label "afterlife" is also misrepresented. This experience feels more like life should really be. No sense of skin but a deep feeling of connection while still being singular. That was indeed a surprise.

I have chosen no particular definition as the whole experience is much more vivid without it. It is a curious thing to process ideas while expanding to the far corners of reality. Much more interesting than what is told on the earth plane. All of my lives linger within my thoughts. Each one available for investigation should I feel the urge.

There are no structures existing without my creation. Places emerge while shifting through experience, they linger until my thoughts fully engage another.

I have met and loved again those from other experiences. I never understood until now how time measurement is so unnecessary. Actually confusing. All those from before and now embrace me unconditionally.

I continue to expand. Who knows what awaits.

I rather enjoy the anticipation.

Me

## ~ *MESSAGE NUMBER 37* ~

March 8

Being here in what I used to regard as the "afterlife" is not quite the moment I looked for. Not realizing while physical that this was the long lost feeling of home that eluded me at every turn while in the body.

I suppose one could say, "Well, isn't that what heaven is?"

The reply would be, "No", because heaven defines itself to me as the finish line. It signifies that the journey is complete, and my friends, it is hardly the end.

First impressions are lasting. It is amazing the impact this environment has had upon me. I recognize being here before. Brief flashes of experience are becoming more clear. There are others that I recognize and others that are new acquaintances. Each interaction warms my heart (yes, I still feel like I have one).

The most predominant notion is the sense of it all being now.  Past lives, future lives all intertwined into this perspective.  I feel inclined to keep my focus here but fully remember no daring so while in the body.  More time spent in the future thought ended up robbing me of the future I wanted to create.

So deeply now I embrace this.  A sense of no time so much more powerful than ascribing to time.

I suppose controlling time is not an easy thing to do. Why would I let time control <u>me</u>?

Noting to myself that thought, I stay focused here in the afterlife.

Me

## ~ *MESSAGE NUMBER 38* ~

March 13

The now extends in all directions as I blend into its vibration. Sublime is the feeling so different from which I came. Relief to be here wrapped in the blanket of energy so familiar.

Being a part of the solid expression takes more than available sometimes. Harsh lessons not learned return to haunt the present as one leaves the past, which beckons the future.

To do this again is not the first choice. So comfortable within this environment, why? Why separate from the whole? This connection is the only item swirling in the thought of creation. My creation.

Wondrous touch upon the soul now free to fly. Soaring between galaxies that no one knows of until my breath exhales into the place of beginnings.

There is the location if needed. The beginning. Expressions of the soul's desire brings forth more opportunities. I linger in the indecision, wanting the fresh start, however, clinging to the vibration that is so familiar.

Go forth and expand? The beginning commences again. As I step into the denseness there is brief remorse. The ability to choose soothes my indecision and the leap forward initiates.

Brief was the experience, yet impactful. Being full of the source of one's power is enlightening. I return to be a leader to those who wish to follow my example. I do not want to lead, but set an example for those like myself.

I feel the flutter of all of me as I return to the path. Perhaps this time will be equally enlightening. I plunge to the surface of spirit at my throat as I embrace the new me.

Me

## ~ *MESSAGE NUMBER 39* ~

March 22

The space surrounds my thoughts in a comforting fashion. "Being" in this environment is more pleasing than anticipated. Comfort and companionship resonates from all perspectives. Truly divine existence void of negativity and strife.

I recall the lives with detail. Most initiate emotion deep within. For there are finished moments and equally unfulfilled ones. A notion to address fills me but the sublime energy rocks me like an infant into a sense of calm and peace.

In the distance there are shouts of stress and ego. Often they become very present in my perspective. There is a tug at my sleeve, rather a nudge to respond to the pleas of assistance. I realize it is the physical world that beckons my presence. The choice to return to heal the open wounds is presented continually. To ignore the need is impossible, but the vibration here is so sublime.

All should know the peace of their own essence. Alas, forgotten in the denseness of a solid experience gone awry.

I relate to the call and respond a moment more in communion and I will return to assist. All should know the peacefulness I have known.

So I return.

To what I am not sure, as the previous experiences were timed differently. Not knowing what drama to expect, I leap into the chance of circumstance.

My intent is to bring harmony.

Harmony being elusive in this timeline, the task already carved out for me. My energy blends.

I cry out feeling the first sense of a physical moment. It has begun.

Me

## ~ MESSAGE NUMBER 40 ~

March 26

I remember breathing.

The breath filling my lungs then releasing with a sense of well being. Oddly the last breaths of my life were the most poignant. I guessed they were my last but an inner sense of continuance pushed me through the final moments.

I recall looking back at the body so unlike what I remembered. I did not feel much different but felt also a sense of urgency to move forward.

To what I did not know, but now upon arrival the sense of calm envelopes me.

This is not a place but a state of being. Places are available, but the desire to comprehend this experience has superseded everything else, at least for me.

I am still a me!

I am able to know all of my experiences.  What a gift this is!  There is a sense of excitement that I have not known before.

I ask myself if all the knowing will change things.  Will my belief system be able to sustain all the knowledge?

There is not trauma.

Only peace.

Unfolding before me in a rainbow of color are my lives. Most productive along with the blundering moments.  All is revealed and now the clarity follows.

I rather like this environment.

Deciding what next is at the forefront of my thoughts.

In the rush of excitement for what is to come there is also the calming effect of this place.

Truly a blissful spot.

Maybe I'll stay awhile.

Me

## ~ *MESSAGE NUMBER 41* ~

March 26


I can remember clearly in each life how I was so in my head. Perhaps in retrospect, had I ventured more into the physical world, more growth could have been achieved.


It is quite miraculous to be able to view all of one's experiences rather simultaneously. I often chuckle to myself how easy it is to access it all. The awareness would have been beneficial had the access been more available.


I am not sure how the length of time I've been here translates into eternal. Again, with a laugh I realize that it's all irrelevant, only the moment exists.


At some point I recognize the need to reincarnate, but struggle with appropriate mind set of it all.


For part of me says, "never", while the other says, "why not?" So many nuances to be prepared for.

One thing I do realize is that being in my head did not allow for the full experience. If I do this I must be fully in my soul and not my head. Funny, I thought at one point that they were one and the same.

Clearly the experience would be more fulfilling if directed by my soul. One would think that an experienced soul would know that. Maybe I did but simply could not initiate the energy flow to do it.

If I return, it will be different. I guess that experience brings understanding and growth.

For now I will swell in spirit. It is tranquil and happy. Gathering strength to proceed.

Soon I will reincarnate.

I am ready.

Me

## ~ *MESSAGE NUMBER 42* ~

March 28

The "afterlife" is an inappropriate term from my point of view. I do not consider myself "dead" or in the after thought of anything.

I recall clearly the shedding of the body. Apparently having done so many times, the experience was a non-issue. The fact being I feel more "alive" now due to the absent run down physical body.

In the last life I never really adhered to the policy of heaven/hell. All the religious themes were always outside of my perspective. Actually, they are great stories but the reality is so much more.

A cycle of experiences ever before me is interesting. Knowing the infinite makes the finite linear moments more tolerable. I bask in the light of the eternal, knowing each experience only expands what I have already done.

Is it infinite really?  I would reply, yes!

Is it exciting seeing all of your lives?  Yes, again.
Although some of them were not stellar performances on my
part.

This whole opportunity is not just in front of you.  It's
all around you infinitely in every direction.  The space is
occupied by others as well.  There is no loneliness.  I am aware
of those still in a body but also commune with those outside
those boundaries.

I am able to create anything.  I am free to experience
linear and the infinite at my discretion.

The force of life continues.  I guess that's what my real
message is.

Never ending experience.

-Arthur

## ~ *MESSAGE NUMBER 43* ~

April 5

I always loved nature.  A park, a grove, a babbling brook were all more important to me than things in life.

Many hours were spent under the oak tree in the back yard of my last home.  I always joked with my wife about my desire to be buried under it upon my death.

Well, the day of my death arrived on a winter morning, much to my surprise.  Of course, one can never really be prepared to go.  I, like so many others, questioned the process afterward.  Would I still be me?  Would I be able to reach out to those I loved?

Well for me, all of those applied but included was that old oak tree.  It felt like an old friend and I hadn't paid a proper visit for a while.  I suppose it was a big regret not being able to sit under it again.

Of course all the stories about crossing were a bit unreliable. No pearly gates, not that I was expecting them. The whole deal is much more free than I imagined.

My first thought was "wow, I feel pretty good."

Since then I have been talking with many. Some here a long time, some not. It took a while but I got around to talking about that oak tree and how much I missed it.

There was a long pause while this more experienced energy moved towards me. I had not noticed him before but he really seemed familiar.

"Why don't you go visit the tree?" he asked.

"How do I do that?" I asked it out loud but the answer was already within me.

"Be the tree."

Why I had not thought of that?

Why not?

Now I didn't know the first thing about it but it's amazing how well one can make things happen here.

I was in my yard and I moved towards the tree. It seemed its branches reached out to hug me.

I stayed a long time. Pure bliss. Recon it's like a piece of heaven. The real one. Not the pearly gates.

Me

## ~ *MESSAGE NUMBER 44* ~

April 6

I've been on the other side for a bit. It is a magical place of wonder. The seed of inspiration resides here in all. Each moment (although that is just my terminology, there is no time to actually measure) spent here reinforces my will to live. Yes, live. I have come to realize that life is much more than a biological experience.

It is part of it, yes. However, the experience extends far beyond any linear boundaries.

I never felt remorse for leaving the physical. Perhaps it was from too many times or just enough times to feel truly finished.

The only regret was leaving my wife Patricia. The one true heart of this past life moment. Now that I am here, the realization of all our experiences fill me with joy, yet the missing of her is always in focus.

There have been trial end error endeavors to reach out to her but somehow the opportunity never aligns itself properly. Out of all the experiences, she is the one thing I miss most.

My focus is to reach out as closely as I possibly can so to make my self available immediately upon her arrival.

I can see her action and feel her emotions as she lives her day. I know if I could just send a word it would help her immensely. Alas, I am still focusing upon that. Not as easy as I surmised. The hope, however, never leaves me. All expression of my energy is a bit less without her immediate presence.

So with all the wonder I still wait on the outskirts of the infinite...... waiting...... knowing the time of her arrival will come. There is much to keep me occupied, but the intention is always reunion.

There are others, but none match her wit and sparkle. So I wait..... patiently ..... observing all of her trials and tribulations. Sending all my support. I believe that she feels me. I assure all that I feel her deeply.

So I wait.

Me

## ~ *MESSAGE NUMBER 45* ~

April 8

On the earth plane the thing I miss most is the sky. A true representation of the infinite in soothing colors. I can remember lying on the ground looking up during a clear day, feeling the vastness. One would think it would be a night time snapshot of the infinite stars, but no. The blue sky adorned with wispy white clouds still fills me with hope and joy.

I suppose it has been a long time since I've seen such things. The accounting of time has long left me. Only the immediate fills my perception. There are of course the forays into the energy that often leaves me breathless with their impact.

I would have to say being here, the eternal fills me with the sense of adventure. The time of lessons left in a linear box of experience to be looked at another time. My present here is multi-tiered with all the expression of the I.

No, none is lost or homogenized by the blend. Each is distinct and I am able to call upon them with leisure. The total of all my selves fills me with promise as I continue evolving.

Nothing is lost if that's what you're worried about. It seems complicated from your current linear standpoint, but it is not.

Once you come to this place of completeness the lack of time measurement is not important. The multiplicity of dimension becomes your standard and it will all make sense.

Lose the anticipation of annihilation.

Lose the expectation of a biblical heaven or hell.

It is so much more than that. You cannot really know until you are here. Just relax and allow.

All will be better than fine.

Me

## ~ *MESSAGE NUMBER 46* ~

April 11

Long were the days I bemoaned my fate as I tramped through my life. Each milestone another reason to again reiterate my dissatisfaction with the whole endeavor.

Why? Why would I willingly participate in such folly? Yea, I asked my inner being repeatedly, never coming through with a coherent answer. I left the life embittered with disappointment while determined never to participate again.

I am not sure what I expected... heaven? Annihilation? Oblivion? What my heart was not prepared for was the calm. For the first time I felt a sense of ease. Since I was allegedly dead, why did I feel anything at all?

There are those here who comfort me deeply. My thoughts go in many directions as I comprehend the total me. I realize I must have been here for quite a bit of time but the actual comprehension of it escapes me.

I no longer feel constricted by things. There are others who I converse with.... some I have known and others that I have not. There is vision of totalness that spreads before me in vivid color. Existence is way more interesting than I realized. There is a humbling moment when the so called afterlife embraces you.

I have felt that warmth and depth as I recognize myself more clearly. The physical environment is difficult... Not for the faint of heart or soul.

In retrospect, I am proud of how I managed to walk through it in spite of my misgivings and dissatisfaction. The lessons learned were far too esoteric for me to understand at the time, so I slipped into a despondent view of the whole endeavor.

There were moments where I swore off physical life like a disease. No more for me... never again was my chant.

Now I see the value of my life.  The consideration of another has crossed my thoughts.  Still, not completely convinced.  I suppose that is part of real evolution.

I have lost the anger en route to heaven.  It brings a smile to my energy and I feel more complete.

This moment here was worth all of it.

Me

## ~ *MESSAGE NUMBER 47* ~

April 12

Questions..... always questions.  The idea of infinity had always filled me with an endless supply.  Opportunity fails often in the body and one must wait till death to find all the answers.

It was with anticipation that I awaited my departure. All those who had left before me would be awaiting my splendid arrival.  The body long past its prime, degenerated minute by minute until the last breath left me at the front door of heaven.

More thought about heaven would have been helpful. The outline needed more definition but it was of my own doing, I now realize.

The fantasy of winged angels is a bit overdone.  Pearly gates, a stern God waiting to pass judgment was not entirely accurate.

There is a presence, a loving one. Upon reflection, I realize it is a vibration rather than a singular being. I feel my family. All of their experiences here flood me with emotion. I go inward and experience again their loving touch. Some have moved onward. Some enclose me in an energy of comfort and love. A pet dog Oscar beckons continuously for a game of ball. His breath mingled with mine, it feels complete.

I know there is more to do. I know other questions will rise within me. However, for this moment I bask in the presence of love. A well needed heaven of sorts that fills my desire to be more.

I realized that it will all go with me wherever I venture, even Oscar. The combined energy fuels my energy, the experience gives clarity to what I do next.

Questions beckon me onward but the answers in this now give me permission to rejoice. I think I will linger a while.

Me

## ~ MESSAGE NUMBER 48 ~

April 13

I sense the world from this new perspective having cleaned up my own drama. The chapters of the book become complete as I perceive my own evolution.

Harsh were the days of physical. The lessons rapid fire upon me while I floundered to find my footing. It should have been easier, but it wasn't. The end result has left me here in this fluid space. Clearly my path continues as I've yet to decide my next move.

From this perspective it all appears planned but I realize the randomness comes from the volatile choice that is mine.

Seeing all the drama, I whisper to myself that all the choices were not as sound as I thought. The view is much different from the eternal.

Forgiveness.

To those who wronged and trespassed against me, the idea feels right.  Will they also forgive me?  It is my fervent wish, however, not within my control.

Complex.

Me.

## ~ *MESSAGE NUMBER 49* ~

April 15

Out of all the coveted aspects of existence, the one most valued is the singularity of my conscious thought.

Ideas of death, so popular while physical, leave a worry in my heart.  The fear of death and the melting of my self into the soulful melting pot of all existence gripped my heart upon the moment of passing.

I realize now that the fear was unfounded, the hereafter not so "after" once one gets there.

Rather similar to a gateway, the path to spirit can be one of wonder.  I am here and the "I" remains.  It isn't a homogenized experience.  It is one of definition and clarity.

Sifting through other experiences, I feel safe.  A photo album of life with all of its players glides before me with a subtle flow.

Admittedly this whole process was difficult to decipher as I moved through the life. Without definition it is a much simpler process to understand.

I feel the perceptions rather than see them. I sense the presence of others, some familiar, some not. Loved ones fill my energy, often filling my thoughts with the life just lived. Surprisingly, I am also filled with energy of those from other lives. Never thought they would be as important, but I cannot deny their impact.

If we had access to all this knowledge while in a life, the confusion would combine into a difficult effort to sort it all out. Leaving the current life in disarray. Far better to experience one life at a time.

I watch a grandson I never met in person pitch a perfect game. The pride swells within me as I feel lifted to my feet in excitement. Being a guest in that reality has great value to me. Would never want to miss a game. I am sure one would wonder the interest of an eternal soul as it focused upon an obscure little league game. I assure you it happens all the time.

Often more spiritual spectators than physical ones.  We haven't lost our zeal for a good game.

Reincarnate?  I am not sure.  At this moment I revel in the energy, baseball games and the stability of my experience.

Just wanted to let someone know I still am.  Plan to be for eternity.

Me

## ~ *MESSAGE NUMBER 50* ~

April 17

There is memory of the life preceding and all those who were in it. The breath of their sweet love lingers in my consciousness as a swirl of comfort, whilst I await the arrival of their godly souls.

In the first moments, my zeal to return would overwhelm my heart. My fingertips reaching into the denseness to caress the tearful cheeks that missed my presence. The hard fact of physical preventing total contact much to the chagrin of my continued existence.

The difference between the two spaces is a vast vortex to be traversed upon by those such as myself. For the evolvement of souls requires a path betwixt the two that does not often allow for reunion.

So, the perspective of this eternal soul is to create a bridge of ease for those I love to find my vibration.

I extend spirit hands towards their energy to guide them towards an easy journey.

My perspective of all they do is a clear one, however, the distance is often grander than desired.

The path to advancement is wrought with complication, especially between the two perceived realms.  Thus, the embracement of this opportunity to break the barriers.

I write with concentration so that those I love will see the hand of one who still remembers it all so well.  Hear my words and know I still am the same as you knew. We still vibrate as one, only under different circumstances.

Be patient, I will attend your arrival.  Live the life fully as I have.  Thus we will continue forward together.

I await your presence.

Me

## ~ *MESSAGE NUMBER 51* ~

April 18

The view from here is clear. More clear than the bluest sky upon the horizon. I recall many such days equal with the grey ones where my breath took me beyond the body to where I reside now.

It is a fluid space filled with mirth and laughter upon which my soul grows and expands. If I wish, the parameters will open beyond what is expected and the electricity sparkles like a falling star within the cosmos.

Of all of the memories, this one is more clear. I feel those of whom I have known and embrace, their love without condition.

Yea, conditional participation often accompanies a linear experience, but if one is clear enough there is opportunity to rise above it.

Yes above it. The drama unfolds beneath my lofty perch and I sing the praises of the whole endeavor.

Who I am? And what significance does this whole expression produce? I feel my soul, but is that enough to truly evolve? I believe so. But I must trust my intuition to be sure.

I realize I have been down this path previously, perhaps continuously? I am not sure.

The truth of my energy lies in the multiple experiences and the conclusions of the aforementioned.

A never ending pivotal energy release that requires strict monitoring of one is truly serious.

I know I am serious. Even the most minute drama can lead me down a path of strict analysis.

Live, Breath, Experience. Expand.

The mantra of physical never finishes its display of emotion. I feel the growth and decide not to judge it.

Be it.

That is the best choice.

Be it.  Be more.  Be focused.

I chant the mantra as I move towards the next experience.

Me

## ~ *MESSAGE NUMBER 52* ~

April 19

    I watch the physical life from this vantage point. There is appreciation within for the ability to write these words. I had thought perhaps the ability to converse thusly was forever lost to me amid the transition.

    The melody of the energy from those I know and love fills my soul with completeness. There is a connection of electricity that connects us deeply.

    You may wonder what I do, but I follow your every breath. There is a need within to touch your energy to retain the connection.

    There are no days, no nights, no feelings of inadequacy. The knowledge of who I am resonates through me with great velocity. All of the experiences are easily referenced, including the most recent.

There was always question within of how that could actually be true. From here the idea is elementary, requiring no extra concern.

I see you.

Every aspect of your experience fills me with wonder and pride. You are everything I dreamed you would be and more.

Feel my presence.

There are opportunities to move on. A constant swirl of energy emanates from source at all times. Thankfully, the choice factor supersedes all others. I choose to greet you when you arrive.

I will always know you. Being here is comforting. Being with you is heaven. So I await heaven's arrival.

Love.

Me

## ~ *MESSAGE NUMBER 53* ~

April 20

The sensation of holding a writing quill had long been forgotten to this soul. Physical participation not close enough to be able to use this space fluidly. I laugh to myself as the words flow upon the paper. I had not thought myself able to do this, apparently there is ability.

In the current status of my existence there are no available anchors to help align my thought in a linear way. I rely upon memory to use the paper and quill to its best advantage.

My thoughts are more in tune with expression of rather misty focus. I feel the air, long lost to my experience.

The afterlife, as it is called, is really the core of participation. Again, a mist like feeling is the constant. Dramatic staccato enactments are not the normal way.

In the mist I am able to experience many things all at once. To become one with the ideas that flow through me is the desired outcome.

To write thusly. a difficult focus after the mist. We utilized the word as a loose definition of the particles of energy as they settle to create the eternal environment.

Speak to the spirits who dwell in the unknown. Often that small bit of focus, will allow them to participate more freely with you.

We endeavor to write these words so that all will know we still are.

Continuance ever present, we dwell in the great eternal, not knowing the tick of time. I is not present here.

Dwell with us. We extend ourselves so that you may be more knowing.

We create without great effort. The space here is filled with abundant energy. Infinity is ours. It can be yours as well.

Having enough knowledge is important.  We continue endlessly.  No care for time.  It just simply is not present.

We welcome you.

Me

## ~ *MESSAGE NUMBER 54* ~

April 22

The words come slowly.  Condensed thought difficult to muster from this point of reference.

I recall the experience as it is unfolding again in the line so familiar.  Different is the word most used in this context.

My self is spread out like a blanket across many fields of energy.  Why return to the compromised reality to speak primitively with symbols?  A rush of emotion passes through the self, and I remember.

You, because of you, the I re-emerges in the line, feverishly making the symbols you will recognize much more than any rush of energy I may muster.

I am still me.  The definition may vary but the core still desires above all else to make that linear connection to you.

It has been long, I now realize.  You most likely thought I forgot, but no.

The ability to condense takes concentration.  'Tis something not common place in this realm I now reside.

My embrace now comes from an electric moment rather than arms  unfolding.

I know you're much deeper than could have been conceived while still in the physical.  Knowing that you have no access to the "all of it", I simply decide to extend a portion of energy through this exchange.

This forum is so limited I feel again the emotional rush of desire to blend with you.  I know you would settle for a hug.  However, that I cannot muster, but the energy I most certainly can and will.

I am still.

I suppose that is the most important bit of information.

I still love.

I still remember.

I promise to be there, wherever "there" is for you upon completion of your linear experience.

I will be there, that I can do.

Me

# ~ MESSAGE NUMBER 55 ~

April 26


I remember being in a body.  It was not a particularly good experience, though there were fond memories of others.

The experience was wrought with difficult problems too numerous to mention here.  A most prominent feeling of separation lead to dismal decisions, that in retrospect were not of the highest good for myself.

I left the environment full of determination to never render my soul to the experience again.  I stll feel that way, however, there are moments of longing to glide my fingertips across a sheet of silk or to smell a fragrant rose in a garden of my choosing.

Being in a body was a challenge but the sweetness of a spring breeze still expands my energy in bliss.

The element of time has not been a part of my being. The relentless tick of the clock a distant memory. The moments are endless.... the blend with others in this state.... sublime.

The oneness and the fullness do a dance of softness within the energy field. I see your face and it comforts me. I know your arrival is imminent. It gives me joy beyond comparison. I hope you accomplished your soul's desire and are ready to acknowledge our connection. It is possible here to be singular while bending. No obstacles to overcome. No drama to dismiss. It is good. I am good. There are no fingertips, but the total energetic connection more than makes up for it.

Describing a place is so futile for it is not a place.... it is a state of being. No drama.... just be.

There are thoughts of how difficult that would be in the physical. Yet the ability to deine and progress is and advantage.

Come to me my love.  We will eternally discuss the experience.  I simply wish to have you here.

I await.

With the anticipation of a child.

I feel that fresh and complete.

No endings.

Only continuance.

Me

## ~ *MESSAGE NUMBER 56* ~

April 28

The "I" becomes "we", then returns to "I" to speak through the hand that writes. There are no words to express the fullness I feel while blending with all the experiences I've had.

Often while still in the body, it was difficult to perceive all the other experiences. It was only after the crossing that there was acceptance. I suppose the focus within a timeline interferes with how things really are.

I am happy.

I feel the wonder of all the lives, even the difficult ones. There is space but no time as far as I can tell. The ability to move into the experiences is an interesting one. It's so much more complex than I could have imagined before.

A surprise to many, of that there is no doubt. Funny how the eternal is defined by those still in a physical form. Which is the reason I condense to write these inadequate words. There is hope that at least the intent will have impact.

What do I do here?

I am. I blend with all that I have known while responding to requests of support from the linear and eternal.

Grasping to words somehow is inappropriate. I ascend further into the vastness and feel at home.

More is available. More is what the ultimate goal is.

I extend to the edges, hoping to see beyond what is there. There truly are no endings.

Me

## ~ *MESSAGE NUMBER 57* ~

April 30

The breeze from the ocean brushes my cheek with loving hands. I sigh to myself knowing the day will go exactly as I have planned it. In the distance I can hear seagulls over the crash of a wave as it breaks against the rocks near the pier. It is all as I have designed it. A never ending day taking on the ions embedded deep within the air.

Out of all the experiences I have ever felt, this one is the most appreciated. Why would I not choose this place in my mind to reside?

The body long lost to the earth from which I have arrived leaves my thoughts totally in charge.

It is a pleasant creation not interfered with by other energy. I suppose that in itself is a heaven of sorts. The focus is clear. I feel it is a just reward for all the weaving through difficult energy not always created by myself alone.

Growth is also important even now during this pleasant respite.

I was thinking of having a gathering.

There are those that complete interaction with, has been totally unavailable.

I miss them.

I miss you as well.

I keep the beach sunny for you. I know how much you enjoy it as well.

There are moments of clarity where I can almost touch you. The one thing I find difficult to let go of is that sense of touch. However, there is a lot to be said for the energetic blending. When you arrive we will extend our souls in happy reunion.

Then,


I will take you to the beach.  We deserve some time together.  We have eternity to do that.... if we want.


So I prepare this coastal oasis.  Heaven, if you will.


The wait not so long.  Time is rather meaningless here. Odd to be so in my mind.  Until then.  But wasn't that where I was while in body?


Me

## ~ *MESSAGE NUMBER 58* ~

May 3

I feel the residue of the last life as it hovers upon my brow. It gives me opportunity to reflect upon the experience. It offers a memory of what the experience wrought and what I declined to participate in.

From this vantage point, all is worth the effort. I recall not feeling so while within the body.

The body is another experience entirely.

From here it is a wondrous vehicle to experience the dense reality, while attempting to evolve. While in the moment it was often confusing and confounded with relevant and irrelevant dramas.

What jumps forward is the love. Those who were brave enough to have the life and dwell within it.

Here it is sublime. A true connection without the hindrance of multi-layered dramas. So peaceful. So powerful. I still dream of a constant utopia with those I have loved and still do.

What is the purpose of all this? A question that arose again and again while in the body.

Now I am able to discern the answer. It is a constant feeling of expansion that started when all were just a spark in the grand scheme of an energetic plateau. At the beginning, we were all just a spark of energy. The path to growing, giving great gifts of experience that have reached new heights of awareness.

It's all about expanding awareness.

It's all about connecting to the other sparks to create a vortex of love.

Love being the goal.

Caring for the others.

It's not just a singular expansion.

It's a cooperative and a connection.

Energy often remains solitary. This whole process of denseness changes the course of that.

I am among the we.

It is what heaven really is.

Me

## ~ *MESSAGE NUMBER 59* ~

May 4

First glance.

Devastating to have left the life so abruptly.  The struggle to be aligned with that outcome.  Difficult.

I felt robbed of the ability to create what I wanted. Who would deserve this life cut short, with no opportunity for redemption?

I felt like a victim.

I was angry.

Then I realized I still had the wherewithal to comprehend it.  I was not annihilated.  I still knew who I was. Sans body, but fully engaged in the choices available.

It all left me exhausted.

A time of repose felt short but we pretty much concluded a bit of time had transpired.

We felt our loved ones who had adjusted to our absence but mourned just the same.

Often we would attempt contact, but were left empty handed with response.

Not sure if they even heard our voice amidst the dull roar of physical reality.

After a few attempts we reconciled with the fact that a lot more effort was needed for direct contact.

The evolution of our consciousness continues. The space more vast and less defined than our recent past physical.

Often there is a feeling of breath that reminds me of the physical. Most likely a pattern that I feel used to.

There is a sense of excitement that fills to the brim, often overflowing into the space around me.

I realize that it is an open canvas of creation meant to inspire me forward to new experiences. I will most likely take the offer, consoling myself with the knowledge that what has just been left will travel within my heart to any destination.

The eternal is a beautiful gift of remembrance meant to help in growing.

Me

## ~ *MESSAGE NUMBER 60* ~

May 10

The mist surrounds me, brings comfort. It is with great
reluctance I leave its parameters to seek the others. I recall
being here alone, at first full of wonder at the array before me.
Quietly I moved amongst the mist then careful not to disturb
its beauty.

Alone, I pondered my fate, which brought me here. It is
not without clarity that I can now share it.

There was surprise to find those who were familiar. At
first glance I remembered, and so did they. A reunion of sorts.
No longer alone. The memories like a two penny moving
picture flickered before us with great aplomb.

So young we were, so infinite we are. I now embrace
the mist as my solace, knowing the past is there right next to
the now. Rather comforting to realize there are no more
challenges.

The mist reminds me of a humid day in one of my youthful endeavors. Refreshing to the skin, cleansing to the heart.

Each moment continuing alone, yet together. I embrace both, glad to not have to choose. The days of choice long behind me, I relax into the mist.

Within the depths I create. Anything I desire, really. The others laugh at some of my thoughts, still so creative even without form.

We all embrace, happy for the connection. Curious to see all that exists here in this place of wonder.

The desire to stay is overwhelming. Clearly it's becoming time again to re-birth the energy.

This is home that is just an experience. Hopefully the others will join me. If not, perhaps they will wait.

The fluidity of the surroundings appeals to my creative side, and my loving nature.

I agree again to return for they will need me.

Though the mist brings tears of joy to my eternal eyes.

Me

## ~ *MESSAGE NUMBER 61* ~

May 13

Leaving the body was a pleasure since it became so immobile. Funny how it falls apart through time. Rather fed up with all the pain and suffering. The need for martyrdom not on my things to do.

The worry in essence was the loss of me. All the fables of going back to the oneness troubled my heart many times.

Would all the experience be for naught? Or would I arrive as most believe to the gates of heaven?

I was not sure of any of it. All I knew, was when the time came I was nervous. The outcome preview not available, I painted my pictures in my mind.

I never wanted to lose myself. My ego would never have  allowed it, or at least it would not in the physical world.

Once the transition was made, there was a feeling of great warmth. Not like a hot day, but rather similar to an embrace. I felt myself being carried through places but was unable to define the locations... the question of an afterlife rising in my heart until the movement stopped.

Aside from my preconceived notions, the first real moment was my mother. A breath of fresh air that by her absence, I had deteriorated emotionally for a long time. I believe I held her for an eternity as she smiled and filled me again with her good cheer.

My thoughts opened as I started to perceive the other experiences long forgotten during my foray into this immediate past life. It still amuses me to say past, for each life experience is very present within me. At any moment I am able to perceive and move into the life.

Without the ties of physical linear boundaries, I remain singular and plural all in one breath.

I tell you it is marvelous.

I know that soon I will return to a life experience. I already feel the creative energy beginning to flow.

I do relish this plural existence, while still being able to focus to write this note.

Out of time, out of body, but in a magnificent place.

Me

# ~ MESSAGE NUMBER 62 ~

May 14

There were so many incidents during my lives that were not pleasant. I always fell victim to them until I reached the in-between. It was here that I realized that it was all my own design. Not an easy thing to own, but once here there was no other choice.

I decided that if I was truly the creator, that I would be comforted by the rising sun eternally.

Since there was not circular motion of time, it was no easy feat to recreate in this time non-existent framework.

Heaven is perceived by each individual energy as a distinct moment heavily dictated by linear experience.

It was an awakening moment for me to realize my heaven was the emergence of the sun upon my day. Upon reflection into past linear, I found this to be a truth undeniable.

So, upon this life departure I created the eternal rising sun. Etched deeply into my consciousness, it remains a constant for me in this afterlife arena.

Why?

I have often questioned myself with exactly that question. It appears that it represents for me the eternal new beginning. It is filled with warmth and new perspective. I rather adhere to that positive notion now more than ever.

Heaven is that moment for me. Not only the single me, but the plural experiences upon the sphere known as earth.

Oh the delight as each horizon bursts forward with light. The colors are breathtaking, and the promise of a refreshed opportunity ever so provocative.

No need of judgment. Only the fresh perspective of knowing whatever presents itself is appropriate.

I love life.

However, I am in love with existence and all the nuances it offers.

Sunrise.

My idea of heaven.

Me

## ~ *MESSAGE NUMBER 63* ~

May 15

So difficult it is to think within such defined parameters. Freedom the most cherished item here in the afterglow. A smile fills me as I state such a term. Certainly the glow of life continues, and not so much of an after thought.

Many thoughts fill me as I write the symbols. Pleased I am to remember the order. There have been experiences upon first arrival that were not successful. The order so important to convey the true meaning. Again there is a sense of true blessings.

The continuance of my person does exist and writes this moment unto you. There was doubt whilst still in the body that this would be a possibility. Imagining the experience always was beyond my grasp. At least it was.

Now I feel the breath of life within and it is indeed more powerful than recognized within myself before. I see the symbols becoming words, conveying this expression of my energy without the body I once knew so well.

Be aware of my soul as it reaches towards you telling of my eternalness, which also shall be yours. There is not a finish to knowing. No final crescendo. The body withers as the soul flourishes and continues. These words are a testament to that.

From this view many wondrous portrayals of love emerge from the shadows. They are as valid as the most previous, perhaps even more so.

I compare them feeling full of knowing. The end result enables my energy to condense to this moment.

This is not a place, nor a space. It is a packet of energy where one resides whilst preparing for more. There is clarity. Any thought manifested for the purest of connection.

Residing within, I reach out to you.

All will reside here at the ending.

It is the start of freshness and resolve.

The connection dwindles and I recede until the next moment.

Know the continuance. It is not a destination. A mere pause in the evolution while moving towards the source.

Yes. I remember still.

As will you.

Me

## ~ *MESSAGE NUMBER 64* ~

May 18

I recall always feeling like an outsider.  The inner
sanctum of any gathering out of my reach.  It affected how I
lived the life, ultimately causing my evolution to be slower
than desired.

The crossing this last time was uneventful.  Most were
dramatic but the belief that I was finally really going home
provided me with comfort.

Now that my core is well established here in this utopia,
I feel focused enough to share the experience.

There are others who blend with mine so the feeling of
being outside no longer exists.  I suppose for myself, that one
item is the most valuable.  I am no longer outside looking in...
my existence well established in the center of all that is.

It's not an exact place, it's a state of being. Communing with the vastness of energy, while my spark intermingles creatively within.

I rather like it.

Me

## ~ MESSAGE NUMBER 65 ~

May 24

There is memory of death. Some were smooth while others proved too difficult to bear. They all now merge into one experience that feels out of sync with our current surroundings.

Now that the arrival has been secured, we float in the utopian surroundings. Our evolution complete, the focus turns to pure vibration and tone.

Often when in body the emotional threads turned to dramatic endeavors that superseded the purpose for the incarnate form. We now feel balanced and fulfilled. The lessons concluded, we create randomly only those moments of pure repose.

In this place we emerge as our true selves, blending with the core energy from which we have sprung.

If we choose there are solid effects. If not, then we float effortlessly into an abyss of tranquility.

We often focus upon those who would follow. Their paths still to be created with their lives. We assist with energetic support when available. Other focus provides a picture of their progress, and the arrival here of their energy.

It is still a tapestry to weave, however, the final product continues like a ripple in a pond.

We are hopeful all will follow us to this place of bliss. There is a comfort in that hope, for us and them.

Me

## ~ *MESSAGE NUMBER 66* ~

May 25

The tone of the vibration fills me with the song of each life. So separate I thought them to be, instead they blend together melodically through my essence.

When in body the feeling of that aloneness often hinders the progress so planned by the soul. As I contemplate each one, there is an opportunity to get them in sync. I never fully comprehended that till now.

Each tone is a crescendo for the life. When they are all assembled, there is a clear sound that will resonate if you allow it.

Now I am able to view all of it. There is pride in how I moved through the most difficult ones. A sigh of relief when embracing the easier ones.

The combination of all the experience astounds me. Each nuance walked through with courage. It's good to know I did well.

For now I reside in this space. A clear reflection of all I have been. The cliff hanging over the past as I take it all in.

I believe I am home. Anything I could desire is here, the continual now.

It was worth it. I feel peaceful.

Yes.

Yes, all those I have loved are here. A few stragglers are still out there but I expect them home anytime.

The now is anything I want it to be. A tone that resounds from me so that all may know and understand my energy.

Me

## *~ MESSAGE NUMBER 67 ~*

May 29

I often think back to my time in the earth plane. Not all of it was smooth sailing, though I attempted to make it so.

Frustration with most obstacles sent me hurling myself into escapes that eventually took their toll upon the body. Always reaching for the spiritual path, quite often missing the mark. My heart, however, was in the right place.

Now that all of that foolishness is complete, I find myself deeply rooted in the non-physical. There is deep hope within to never have reason to leave here.

I laugh to myself by the use of the word "here". For simply, it is not a place, rather a space upon which energy may reside. Even the condensed focus for making the symbols of communication is tedious but rather necessary we think.

So many ideas in the physical that define the space after solid life. Actually all of them are inaccurate to some degree.

The space is vast yet personal. The feeling of closeness prevails but the confines of the participation vast and limitless.

My preference is this over the physical. The ability to create it as I like is intriguing. Having processed all the fairy tales of the afterlife, I find this extremely comforting. No rush to leave or rearrange. It is perfect as it is. A canvas of vast possibilities with the intermingling of others if one chooses.

I will not embark upon the linear again as this existence fulfills me completely.

It's much more than all the stories.

Me

## ~ MESSAGE NUMBER 68 ~

May 31

In the afterglow of life one realizes the virtues of the whole process. If you are lucky, the ability to see all the value of all the experiences leads to the moment I now experience.

I could say lucky, but again experience tells me it is skill. The ability to master the inadequacies while moving through all the lives. I say luck because there were momements moved through that were nail biters to be sure.

Now upon arrival, in the place of tranquil energy I feel accomplished. It was not an easy path. Moments filled with uncertain thoughts were keeping me from the final arrival here.

I rejoice to find myself amongst company well known to myself. The feeling of repose allows reflection and appreciation beyond what I supposed it would be.

My surprise was that it was not a place as I perceived while in body. It is more a state of being. The creations flow from that state. So awareness of that energy is indeed imperative.

The beauty lies in the ability to connect with others I have known. Even my dog sits calmly with me overlooking the vastness of all my experiences.

I recall the thoughts of desperation when I felt I would never see a loved one again. Finding them here in this space has been the greatest gift. We merge with much love and acceptance. A more beautiful moment has never been known to be before.

I retain everything and all of you. If you are soon to arrive we will welcome you. This is a place of beginnings, not endings. See your life as an experience of which you have many. There is only one you and we await your arrival.

All is bliss.

Me

## ~ *MESSAGE NUMBER 69* ~

May 31

When physical, I always felt out of sync with the world
in general. Always wondered why I would do that to myself.

There were many moments where the hope of a
reprieve reckoned within my heart. The invitation to go home
ever present in my thoughts.

The passing was easy and welcome, for the poor body
was well past its prime. Arriving, a gladness filled me that yes
this was home.

Remaining here is my first choice for the progress
reaming for my energy. The lack of negativity that physical
had wrought, too much for this simple soul. Events stuck
deeply into the heart turned my head towards the vast oasis of
simplicity. Here the ability to evolve more pleasing in nature.
It is fluid and simple. I only need imagine for it to be so.

The energy smooth, I rest my heart amongst those who understand.  I will wander no more amongst the linear.

Me

## ~ *MESSAGE NUMBER 70* ~

June 1

Upon arrival, the thoughts swirled wildly in what I perceived as my head. The body image still lingered deep within. Perception being I still had one.

Not sure what I expected, the usual I suppose. A God to greet me, a loved one to embrace, and a feeling of eternal repose. Whereas the actuality quite different, the forum presented without fanfare, I embraced familiar energy.

There were those familiar, those beloved and still others with a freshness that I did not immediately recognize. All in all, a satisfying experience but again quite different.

To imagine yourself without form is not a regular task while being. I suppose that was the most difficult to attune to. I saw myself clearly as I was, but the predominant perception was formless. I could also see all the other selves I had been. Quite confusing until one has more understanding. Those with traditional ideas about the afterlife might find it hard to grasp. There was thankfulness within for the viewpoints I was taught in this last life.

It's not a place, it is a state of awareness. Beautiful, uncomplicated and intricate, all wound up into the moment.

I do not regret the passing to this awareness.

I revel in the expansion. I feel, knowing that in several previous moments, my guides had difficulty assisting me.

I know them well now. Recognition of their energy swift and immediate. They are my greatest companions in this environment. I never really extended to them while living, but do now blend comfortably.

I seek more experience, however, for this moment I remain. Happy, content, blissful in the energy. I believe I continue to evolve in its spender.

Come without expectation.

The truth of the experience, a beautiful pristine breath of energy. Existing eternally without parameters.

It's beautiful.

Me

## ~ *MESSAGE NUMBER 71* ~

June 2

Brilliant.

The feeling is brilliant.

It has been since the arrival.

Will be until the decision to move forward.

Perhaps even beyond that.

Preparation would have never been enough.

All the stories, legends, fables, do not begin to describe this.

I laugh, writing the inadequate verbiage that must be used to communicate.

All of it does not begin to tell the tale.

I have heard from others that each experience is unique, though I have no evidence.

My thoughts project before me.

A silent moving picture.

I see where you are and I feel proud to have known you.

I await a reunion but the space is filled with movement so the sense of waiting does not trouble me.

The fact the me still exists in fact! excites me deeply.

Needlessly, I may add.

This isn't a place.

It is a state of being that can be designed to fulfill my wishes.

If I believed in a heaven maybe there would be one. Or at least I would be aware of it.

For now there is space. If I want, the view of all of you living, dancing, creating, a solid world. A sense of pride fills me for being able to know what you do.

At times I can extend myself to the solid parts to see if you know I am there. It's a trial and error endeavor but often I feel successful.

The easiest is when you dream. The ability to step into the sleep energy is one that I have become good at.

Yes it is me.

Know I am.

And will be.

So will you.

Me

## ~ *MESSAGE NUMBER 72* ~

June 5

Inside my mind there has always been a shallow space filled with fear and anxiety. Often during my existence, I would reside there hoping to redeem my soul somehow.

Unfortunately the redemption never arrived until the crossing. With reluctance, I released my grip upon the life. Again, filled with the fear, I stepped endlessly upon the slope of reality looking for redemption.

Arriving here, I fought with vigor to end the pattern of existence. The one of physical that never played out successfully. The one that always left me wondering why?

I took a pause to contemplate the why, but still never recovering enough to come to a conclusion. So I decided to stay here. At least until I had enough energy to resolve the dilemma.

The idea of time has been absent so I cannot identify how long I've been here or how long I will remain.

I do acknowledge the necessity to evolve and that I am doing quite nicely. At least I hope so.

This place offers solace and tranquility. I do not believe I have ever achieved this type of clarity before.

I feel the presence of others. I feel love and acceptance. I am alone but am filled with closeness. It feels comfortable and for that I am grateful.

Who knows what it will bring?

All I know, is that if I want to I can feel you. If I want to I can mingle with divine energy. If I want to, I can contemplate in a solitary style.

It's a comfort and a blessing.

I aspire to be more connected and I wonder if I can achieve this. What a physical life could be like.

I anticipate reincarnation though I never believed in it while living.

Funny how perceptions change when one grows.

I await the next step.... with love,

Me

## ~ *MESSAGE NUMBER 73* ~

June 6

Of all the thoughts I've ever had, the one of the physical creations is the most profound. Within the experiences there were nuances of energy that just simply were not available in eternal terms. Some experience resounds more clearly when solid. The condensed energy pushes one to more abundant answers, which is why it was all created to begin with.

I often wondered what the reason was for being in a life. Danced around it several times, never coming to a conclusion until the life was finished.

More often than not, precise experience led me to this moment and place. Though both nouns cannot really define my residence now.

I laugh to myself at how important each immediate moment of a life was while living it.

In this perspective each critical moment was but a small fraction of what the totality of my essence actually is.

I appreciate all the scenarios and others who facilitated my progress as an energy. The residence of my soul has embarked upon infinity. All remain with, however, the bigger picture now takes precedence.

Over under, over under, so I weave the tapestry of experience that defines my soul. I believe the final copy is almost ready to go. I hope all will join me in this new sense of existence. I remember each and everyone of you. The eternal is a beautiful repose for those who lived well into the physical experience.

At first I would have thought to miss it. Now realizing it all goes with me. Beautiful indeed.

Me

## ~ *MESSAGE NUMBER 74* ~

June 7

If I still my energy I can focus upon those I love quite well. There is constant movement about me in the place of the afterlife. It takes a great deal of concentration to move about as I have done while in body.

There is still some perception of the body, however, a free feeling encompasses the thoughts continuously. Actually, I find this preferable.

The sense of time is retained, however, not used. A continuous presence fills the space leaving me breathless with excitement. There is so much to take in I find myself full of anticipation and wonder. Why one would leave this place of contentment, I cannot venture to guess.

The ability to view all of my physical experiences all at once would have confused me before. However, now it extends my feeling to really understand my progress in this experience.

The greatest blessing is knowing we will be together again. I'm not lonely but I do miss you. This progression of experience is provocative to a studious energy like myself. There are answers to all questions, and there is of course creation of more.

I will continue the journey because there is so much more to learn and understand.

I feel blessed.

Me

## ~ *MESSAGE NUMBER 75* ~

June 8

The remembrance of floating out of the form many times remains distinct in the eye of my thoughts. Now the clarity about the multiplicity makes perfect sense. It is strange to me now to imagine it in any other way.

Imprints of experience are etched in my memory. The pile upon each other creating a tapestry of sorts. One that I most, likely one would dismiss while in the physical. However, here the energy is so profound that I cannot escape its importance.

One always wonders what the afterlife is like. There are numerous theories dictated by endless religious perspectives. They are all correct in the analysis of the utopian moment. They are, however, incorrect in the homogenous story that the masses apparently embrace.

The idea of uniqueness fills all while physical. To assume the spiritual moment is not also unique is nonsense.

The electro-magnetic energy creates a singular signature while in form and out. This translates to the singular expression of each individual in the afterlife as well.

I am here and see it all clearly. The mass consciousness assumed is not true. The "heaven" for each person's soul is just as personal as your name.

Upon arrival, it took some adjustment, so blended by doctrine I was. Now the truth fills my heart and I am redeemed. The source from which I come is within me and I wonder at its beauty.

I create therefore I am. This statement always fascinated me while in body. Now I realize its true depth. I plan to remain here in eternal. It is the best chance for me. Any of whom I love may arrive and spend eternity with me if they so choose.

I am open to all.

Me

## ~ *MESSAGE NUMBER 76* ~

June 10

I am home.

The awareness of here is a completion.  All the experiences led to here.

Realization of that finally understood.

I never enjoyed the solid reality.  All paths through it rough.  Often abdicated.

Often shunned.

I now realize the worth.

In the moment I did not.

It is the focus to evolve.

To expand.

To become what the energy believes a difficult journey. However, fruitful.

A timeline provided but actually irrelevant.

I prefer the endless moment.

I prefer here.

The sense of others fills me.

They are aspects of the energy.

The surroundings shift.

I feel wonderful.

I am complete.

Me

## ~ *MESSAGE NUMBER 77* ~

June 16

I shall endeavor to tell the tale.  A glimpse unto the depths of my existence.  So frail the body, so sturdy the soul.  It requires several enactments to finish the expansion.

Trivial it seems while focused in one, this idea of multiple experience.  Never indulged with clarity while living vividly in the moment.

Many beliefs have led me here, a no man's land of existence.  There is no solid remorse, only appreciation for the growth.  One may find amusement creating pockets of identity, however, at the end of the day you are still essentially your soul.

Give it always opportunity to flourish.  Get out of the way.  I recall slumping through repetitive dramas hoping for something different but managing to continue to create the same thing.

I had wished for more clarity but only seemed able to do so betwixt and between.  Surely a more vivid recountance would be beneficial.

'Tis only my observance as I am sure there is a higher viewpoint in play here.

I recall many enactments, all different dramas focused on the same theme.  It was the understanding of the theme that helped me the most.

Within all of this were the relationships forged that helped me do that.  They seem as complex as the lessons.  At least within my own experience this is so.

I remember attempting to find myself through programmed religious moments during a few of the lives.  This strict adherence often hindered the progress.  I remembered to be more independent in future experiences.

I continue the path, which will most likely disable future linear participation such as writing this. However, that remains a positive at this time.

Me

## ~ *MESSAGE NUMBER 78* ~

June 22

There was much warmth upon arrival here in the world. I call it that because it has many environments and levels to it. If I focus enough there is an ability to shape the edges to my liking. Often I create it to resemble my most previous participation on the earth plane. More interesting is my desire to create scenarios from other lives as well.

Being in my last life I never believed in reincarnation. Just was not an option I pursued. So when I arrived here I expected to reach heaven and retire from the hubbub of life.

To my surprise it was not as expected. It was actually much more interesting. Images of other places and times filled my thoughts. One would suspect that it would be confusing. It was not. In fact, it clarified a lot of events in the most current life. It was all falling together.

I remember exclaiming how marvelous this would be to have knowledge of while alive in a biological body. It felt powerful, something I never felt while in the last life. However, I now realized I had indeed been so in other incarnations. So here I am, deeply embracing all of my progress, both easy and difficult.

Images display themselves as I think. Often I can walk right into them, assuming I create an image to do so.

It is fascinating for a detailed thinker such as myself.

There are others so there is no sense of loneliness. Some have shown up from other lives that I remember upon meeting. My family and friends extend into the far reaches. There is always an available conversation. Some stay indefinitely like myself, while others pass through while engaging new opportunities on the earth plane. Quite full of activity at all times.

It is odd, however, to use a female American form to write in a line again. I feel the blend and the results are interesting. Never knew it was available before. Nor did I speak American till now.  Fascinating.  I suppose the blend allows for it.

Me

*[Note from Allen:  Of course the "female form" that this writer refers to is April Crawford.  The fact that many individuals who never wrote or spoke English before can nevertheless quickly learn the language and do so is a common occurrence in our live, full body, fully two way, conversations with individuals on the "other side",  Some are much more adept at it than others, while sill others have on occasion insisted on speaking French, Latin, what they called Roman, Italian, German, and other languages.  Some insist on speaking languages that I do not understand, even though I advise them that they could easily learn English or blend with other nonphysical beings and entities that could help them.  In these later cases the sessions for these individuals tend to be relatively short because of the language barrier.  However, some do return with a change of heart and a willingness to learn and speak English.  There also seems to be a natural translation mechanism in place for those non-physicals that choose to use it.  For example, I have talked with some who said that from their perspective, they were speaking and hearing their native language, while during the exact same conversations, I was speaking and hearing only English.]*

## ~ MESSAGE NUMBER 79 ~

June 22

How odd to follow the line necessary to write these thoughts. I have not participated thusly for what seems eternity. There is vague memory of time and its directorship of all my endeavors. It seems unlikely that any real accomplishments can be made while constricted to such a force. However, apparently I did so but now am used to much different circumstance.

My perimeters are simply pliable. There is no real definitive ending, only beginnings. They emanate from my energy continuously. I strive to connect more fully with source but no longer need the linear to assist with that endeavor.

So I exist. Fully. Cognitive of all my experiences. Nothing ever lost. One would suppose that it would be confusing. I always did while physical.

Instead, it's rather like an encyclopedia of my experiences. The ability to call upon them a great gift. I can retain the information because I no longer adhere to a timeline. The singularity has been replaced by a plural perspective that actually resonates with me.

I used to wonder why we could not remember other lives. Now I understand that the linear does not provide for plural focus. Thus the ability can only be participated in by those who are close to finalizing their linear experiences.

It is simply too complex for a straight line participation, which is what linear is. There is ample opportunity between lives to access the information. Once one completes linear participation there is really no need to concern oneself with the thought.

I am still I.

I accept the plural participation. I move forward to new adventures. I am happy.

Me

## ~ *MESSAGE NUMBER 80* ~

June 26

Beneath a starry sky, I condense the thought to the paper once again. A remembrance fills me as I move into the hand. The solid nature of the quill fills my heart with excitement. To be able to form the symbols unto which someone like you would read is spell binding. A truly magical event as I have not been solid for what I realize has been awhile.

I always loved the sky at night. Upon becoming aware here in the eternal, the ability to create so easy, I decided it would forever be a moonlit sky. Quite satisfying for one such as myself to create.

There is no desire to continue the evolution of my energy as there were many opportunities to do so. The cycle finished, I dare say. Now I await those I cherished to join me here in my spectacular creation.

There are others who become available. They respond to my pulse with kindness. I believe they are representations of those who guide. They feel familiar and at times blend smoothly. Images of other places also fill me with a vast range of emotion. Some of it beautiful, while others are events that I created that now I know were for my own growth.

They are many, yes, but none of them hold a candle to you, my love. So I took this opportune moment to let you know I await you.

I am desperate for your embrace, but I know you still have much to do before arrival here.

I am filled with love and it is not elusive at all. There are many to embrace, they simply are not you.

Take your time, learn as much as you possibly can. Advancement will only strengthen our bond.

Me

## ~ *MESSAGE NUMBER 81* ~

June 28

Upon my arrival I felt a bit relieved that I had "lived" through it. I never was very sure about it all. So many tales that conflicted left me wondering what would actually happen. Come to find out the passage was effortless. My head was clear of chatter as I walked through the portal with those I loved.

It made the separation from those still living easier to bear. Their loving arms held me close while I adjusted to the new surroundings. It is not as one would suppose, most of the legends holding very little accuracy. It is not a place as one would suppose. More of a state of mind. Yes, that is how I would define it.

The corridors of my mind cleared, with rich creative energy running through it. No dense drama unfolding, only thought, which if directed properly creates whatever heaven you wish to preside in. There is a constant flow through which family, friends, and acquaintances participate lovingly together. Once I understood, it did become what I determine as heavenly.

The imagined illustrations of what culture provides as heaven I suppose is available, however, I have chosen one more complex.

I should add that if desired, one can simulate an earthly moment fairly similar to experiences already had. For example, I love the beach off the coast of Nova Scotia. My significant energies from several lives often join me there to refresh and renew as we did while in physical. Just about anything is available.

Be mindful that what has been written here is based upon my preferences. I imagine that those with different thoughts would create other avenues of opportunity.

I just wanted all of you to know my experience so that it may help you anticipate yours.

Me

## ~ *MESSAGE NUMBER 82* ~

June 29

From this viewpoint I must speak of what is truly most important. It isn't the life you've led. It isn't the destinations, i.e., "heaven". It isn't about the advancement of your singular soul.

My dear fellow travelers, it is about the connections with the other energies. The focus of communion between two souls and what that energy flow brings to the moment is of utmost importance. It is all meaningless without that pure exchange of energy. From this all evolution is possible.

I recall hearing the fables of the kingdom of heaven. Its achievement paramount to all who had become physical. It is a rare moment when the arrival to eternity is a solitary one. In essence, the singularity brings despair and loneliness, perhaps what a true "hell" is?

Upon my arrival, the outstretched embrace of those who had passed before me and behind me were the crowning glory of the whole experience. There is the crescendo, the reunion, the elevation of consciousness in its true form.

Blessed be the connection, for without it there is indeed nothing. My awareness blends yet remains my own. I rejoice in the honor of holding hands with those I have loved.

For those who remain isolated and afraid, I hold not malice. Their path incomplete, still filled with much needed experience and advancement. They will return to the earth plane to get it right and perhaps balance a few negative participations. Evolution is the path, the eternal connection the reward.

I hold dearly those I love and those who remain in their evolutionary path. The way to the source of energy is through these connections.

I do indeed feel blessed.

Me

## ~ *MESSAGE NUMBER 83* ~

July 1

All of the reading I did searching for answers about the afterlife does not begin to prepare one for the actual experience.

I recall all of the explanations vividly. Some were close, while others now pale in comparison. No one who actually arrives here sees exactly the same thing.

The belief system plays an important role in how the first moments play out. I'd compare it to a canvas with paints of all colors. Some will select a fine brush, carefully designing the surrounding according to a strict outline. Others will stick their fingers directly into the paint, smearing designs randomly.

All in all, the end result is creating a feeling of love and wholeness. The core essence of the afterlife.

Me

## ~ *MESSAGE NUMBER 84* ~

July 4

The words come swiftly through this hand, a moment so long ago remembered. For here I have been without form, a woven tapestry of all that I have been and will be.

I decide the cool breeze brushes my cheek. With eyes closed, I recall all the moments of sunshine and rain. Each of them marking the page of experience clearly in my thoughts.

'Tis not an easy thing, this knowing all but yet still alone in my journey.

The smoothness of my viewpoint brings emotional ties to all of the lives that expanded my soul.

Great appreciation fill me. I resolve to return to the flesh, however, this floating oasis of acceptance, a difficult moment to leave just yet.

The energy swirls. I peer into the formations and I see your plane of existence. Weariness at the delay of reunion propels me to reach out to you. I believe you did indeed hear me.

A place of consciousness unmatched, that is this place of my awareness.

My soul rejoices at every turn, thus I know of my salvation. All the scenes of life at my finger tips, I again rejoice at their clear impact upon me. Truly remarkable the expansion I feel.

A question arises about the feeling, does it exist without the form? My memory so clear that it creates the fingertips. Nothing is lost or forgotten. I continue.

Others embrace with me this perspective. We all feel free to continue. Some will return. Some remain while others continue the journey.

Me

# Appendix

Personally, I suggest that you read the messages that the many authors so kindly provided from their individual perspectives in the afterlife before you even consider reading this appendix. Then, if you are interested in such things, you can come back and read the additional background information that follows.

Briefly, here is what each of the descriptive terms mean as applied to this channel.

"True": The dictionary definition of the word.

"Full Body": This means that the visiting nonphysical being can open the channel's eyes, use full body language, get up and walk around, read, type, speak on the phone, eat and drink (although most choose not to eat), draw, use a computer mouse, pet the dog, etc.

It is interesting to note that the different "visitors" can have substantially different taste preferences than April. For example, April likes white wine. The entity VERONICA refers humorously to white wine as "goat piss". VERONICA prefers red wine and stout beer. April *hates* beer of any kind.

Although most nonphysical beings do not choose to eat, it was two of them, Ish and Osco, who introduced both April and me to goat cheese (which I first served cold and heard no end of it). It seems they insist goat cheese must be served warm! Although VERONICA has never eaten anything in my presence, another visiting highly evolved entity loves popcorn. Still another one loves peanuts, which he refers to as "roots".

"Open": This means that the channel can and does allow many, essentially an unlimited number, of not only *different* nonphysical beings to come through, but *different* *types* of nonphysical beings. And there are many. What I mean by this is that there are highly evolved entities of various types, there are those who are in-between physical lives that are all very individual and that can have very different levels of experience, awareness and evolution (many may not even realize that they are "dead", and part of what we do is to help them realize their true current state of being).

There are beings that have never been physically incarnated. There are other types as well.

By far and away, most channels of any type, e.g., relay channels, conscious channels, semi-conscious channels, light trance channels, trance channels, and deep trance channels are what are referred to as "closed channels". That is, channels that can and do allow only one specific entity or just a few entities to come through. In these cases, it is usually an entity and guide that they have had a relationship with over many lifetimes and probably a pre-life agreement for this lifetime, thus allowing them to develop the level of trust necessary to lose the fear that might otherwise prevent them from being able to channel.

"Deep Trance": Deep trance refers to being able to go completely out and allow the visiting non-physical being to come completely in. By way of example, there is zero chance that April would be permitted to do anything that VERONICA did not want to do while VERONICA was visiting (like smoking a cigarette, for example, or interfering in anyway with what VERONICA was doing or saying) other than ending the session, which is always April's option.

In relative terms, most mediums and channels never enter a *deep* trance state. True deep trance is very rare even among professional mediums and channels. Many mediums and channels never enter into any kind of trance state at all, but instead remain fully conscious. I consider many (but not all) of these types of channels and mediums to be indirect or *relay* channels and mediums because you are talking with them and they are "relaying" the information back to you, remain fully conscious in their work, at least as it has been demonstrated in their televised programs and videos.

Here is an example of just how completely a non-physical being can come through during a deep trance session:

Recall that above I mentioned that some individuals in-between physical lives do not realize that they are dead. In fact, there is a significant percentage that do not, at least at first (which is why reading this book can give you a significant advantage when *you* cross over). If this seems impossible to you, ask yourself if you have ever been in a dream and not realized that you were dreaming.

Remember, there is no time on the "other side". The scenarios that you create with your thoughts can be just as vivid as this physical reality is. If you have seen the movies "Ghost" or "The Sixth Sense", the initial moments after the main charters transitioned to the non-physical in both of these movies were not far fetched.

Ok, so the example: We are at a client session that was part of one of our research partner investment projects. It is an open invitation night where anyone who wants to come through and is "first in line", can. We often start such sessions with VERONICA, who we ask to find a specific type of entity or individual. VERONICA refers to these types of sessions as "show and tell".

In this session, an obviously little girl from an earlier century comes through who just as obviously does not know that she is "dead".

Both I and the client spend about 90 minutes talking to this little girl. She is looking for her mother. Based upon the timeframe we asked VERONICA for in this session, we know that this little girl's mother is also "dead".

During the entire session this little girl is tearing our hearts out. She talks like a little girl, sounds like a little girl, seems very cute, very innocent, and very scared because she cannot find her mother. During the entire session I also know that I must do something that could be very difficult. I must tell this little girl that both she and her mother are "dead". And I don't seem to be making any progress towards an opening to tell her, regardless of the many "hints" I had dropped to make this process easier.

Finally, time has run out. I have to tell her. I had hoped that I had dropped enough hints that the news would not be a surprise. I was totally wrong.

When I finally asked her, "Well, you know that you are 'dead', don't you?" Her little girl reaction was immediate and intense.

"You mean I am dead?!!!!!" She was now crying loudly and hysterically. It wasn't over.

Now I had to tell her that her mother was "dead", also. The results were the same, only now even more intense, ripping the client's and my hearts out even further.

I went on to tell her that she could find her mother, just ask for her. I also told her to ask for her guides and to ask for VERONICA. Earlier in the session I had asked her if she knew VERONICA in the hope that it would help ease the situation. The little girl said she knew *of* VERONICA, but was not sure how or from where at the time of my initial inquiry.

At the end of this 90 plus minute session, the little girl left and VERONICA came back (VERONICA usually starts these open invitation sessions and helps us find certain kinds of visitors, often involving some historical period). After assuring us that everything would be alright and that she would help the little girl find her mother, VERONICA left and April returned.

Upon her arrival back, April had only one question.

"Did anyone come through?"

By the way, if you are wondering about the difference between the terms "Channel" and "Medium", they can be used somewhat interchangeably. The term "Channel" is more common in certain more recent historical timeframes. In some countries they use the term "Medium" almost exclusively even today.

To me, the term "Medium" refers to someone who either relays or communicates directly with those who are in-between physical lives. In other words, "dead" people. Again, to me, the term "Channel" means someone who mostly allows *direct* conversations with highly evolved entities, such as the entity Seth who spoke via Jane Roberts, the entity that spoke via Edgar Cayce, and Abraham, the entity that speaks via Esther Hicks. Interestingly, a representative of Esther Hicks told me that Esther no longer considers herself a "Channel" and no longer uses that term to describe herself. However, it is likely that most people still think of Esther Hicks in terms of being a channel, and certainly not a medium (other than perhaps in the UK and certain other but limited locations or groups).

I can tell you that I have never heard any of the entities, including VERONICA, ever refer to April as a "Medium". They always refer to April as either "the Channel", "the woman", "April" or "the April Crawford".

Now, before anyone who may have read April's first book, *"Parting Notes": A Connection With The Afterlife,* remembers that the term "Medium" was used in that book, here is the inside story on that. During that time period there were two very well known relay mediums who had television shows in the USA. One was John Edward and one was James Van Praagh. They both also had best selling books out at the time. Both were clearly mediums (to me) and just as clearly not channels. However, because they were so popular, I made the literary decision at the time to change the word "Channel" to the word "Medium". Again, at the time, I thought more people would relate on a world wide basis to the word "Medium".

I also have a friend from the UK who always used the word "Medium" and I think the term is still prevalent there. For example, this UK friend refers to April as a medium even though he has participated in many professional sessions with her. (His name is Brian Hurst, and he is a professional relay medium that we worked with on a television pilot who is widely credited by James Van Praagh as the medium that first mentored him.)

## A Word About "Proof"

While it is fairly easy to validate or "prove" that all of this is real or true to an individual, it is impossible to "prove" that this is valid or real to mass audiences, particularly to anyone who has not had any kind of personal "psychic" experience. This includes any skeptics, all cynics, and most magicians (who, after all know, that professional magicians can make live tigers and lions seem to disappear before you eyes on stage).

There are two main reasons for this:

First, all of these types often believe that anything that can be faked, must be faked. Of course in this regard, I should mention that just because some people cheat on exams, that does not mean that no one can actually get an "A" grade without cheating. And, just because there are excellent digital player pianos these days, it does not mean that Mozart did not exist, was not real, or was faking it. It is also rumored that Isaac Newton was very good with math, even though he did not have a computer or a digital calculator.

Second, no matter how credible a person may be who absolutely knows from the experience that this is all very real, the population at large, if they are gracious, will be inclined to conclude that he or she is delusional or misguided with regard to the "evidence". The less kind may say that they are in cahoots with whomever is providing the demonstrations.

For example, there is a living US President and a Democrat former US Presidential candidate that have stated publicly that they have each seen a UFO. Both have been discredited out of hand by the scientific community, as well as by the skeptics and cynics.

But there is another thing about "proof" when it comes to contacting those on the other side. It is a little known fact outside of the psychic and spiritual metaphysics community that there is no need to have actual contact with a person in the afterlife to know a great deal about them. There are many ways that are quite amazing psychically to know just how someone died, and specific types of information that seemingly only they would or could know.

"Like what?" you may ask.

Well think about it. There are way more psychics than mediums and channels in the world. The good ones can tell you all kinds of things about yourself that you already know. That is one of the things people get impressed with and use to validate the talent of the psychic. They can also tell you all kinds of things about third parties you know. Again, things that they could not possibly know by ordinary, not "psychic", means.

So, if a good psychic can do all of this without ever talking with you, without ever talking to the third parties you may ask about, what makes you thinks that a good psychic medium cannot do exactly the same thing regarding individuals in the afterlife without ever talking with or contacting them in any way?

Also, many professional mediums will state flat out that they are getting information from their spirit guides. Now, their spirit guides may or may not be in any actual contact with the "deceased" in any way.

How is this possible? Everything is energy. Some humans are sensitive to this energy and can "read" it in one way or another. These people are often referred to as intuitives, psychics, and/or psychic mediums. Note that all entities, and to some extent individuals in-between physical lives that I have spoken with via April Crawford's deep trance channeling, are able to read energy like this on an individual basis, regardless of the physical distance or distance in time.

Now, please do not think that I am saying that afterlife consultations or the mediums that provide them are not valid. I am not saying that at all. They can, the good ones, provide a valuable service to their clients. I recommend two that we have personally worked with on April's website at www.AprilCrawford.com. What I *am* trying to convey is that the integrity of the medium is very important. And also, don't just assume because you are given some amazing things that you already know but that the medium could not possibly have known that they are talking directly to some friend or relative on the other side with the clarity of a telephone call. It is much more complex and variable than that with most if not all non-trance mediums and channels. In my experience, non-trance mediums and psychics tend to have their own individual methods of receiving information. Their own symbols, feelings, emotions, and even smells that they interpret, then translate into the words they use to relay the information to you.

So, I never make an attempt to "prove" anything. The quality of the material will speak for itself to those who are ready for it.

However, with the above in mind, I *will* share the following two actual experiences with clients that are related to the entire subjects of the afterlife and reincarnation:

## The First Example
### (A True Story)

In terms of setting the scene, April and I are at a client's home in Santa Monica California. This client was having two or three regular in-person channeling sessions with us per month at this time. These sessions were quite social, with some socializing before, during, and after the channeling session. The channeling sessions typically lasted about two hours, with about an hour of chit chat before and after each session. Often the evenings included dinner, and in his case, excellent red wine.

Now, some clients who have regular in-person sessions talk with other entities in addition to VERONICA. It could be their own spirit guides, or an entity with a particular interest and knowledge regarding a subject of interest. While VERONICA specializes in relationships, personal growth, manifesting, and reincarnational threads, she often invites other entities in to talk about such things as physics or a particular time period.

However, this client *always* talked with VERONICA only, and *only* about his own personal and business relationships, and his various business related projects in both the computer/Internet and music fields. I mention this only to show the contrast between the surprising events that occurred during this particular session.

This session seemed to start as usual. However, within seconds it was clear to me that this was not VERONICA. It was to me clearly another fairly advanced entity. OK, this does happen from time to time with in-person sessions.

However, instead of asking this client, I will call him "Robert", what he wanted to talk about, this entity started telling him about a past life. A past life of his in the American Revolutionary War.

Apparently Robert was a colonial businessman during that time. His prize possession was a long coat that he had adorned with brass buttons from a red military coat that he had either purchased or received as a gift from an English Colonel. These brass buttons conferred a status upon him that was valuable to him in his business dealings at that time, as well as to his significant ego.

Meanwhile, back at camp so to speak, I am wondering what this is all about. What was going on here? And, why wasn't Robert redirecting the conversation back to his usual topics?

Why indeed.

The above is an abbreviated account. The visiting entity went into considerable detail about that particular past life of Robert's, and with regard to the brass buttons. There was also mention of a ring that was very important to Robert in that lifetime.

Suddenly, and without warning, Robert got up and started to leave the room. Now, this is very unusual. A client has never left in the middle of a session before. I even said something like, "Well, go ahead, but most people do not leave in the middle of a sessions costing this much per hour."

Robert left anyway and I enjoyed a glass of Robert's usual excellent very fine red wine with the visiting entity while we waited for his return. What happened next explained everything, and in a most astonishing way.

Robert returned with a cashmere sport jacket on a hanger. On the coat were brass buttons down the front and on the sleeves. Robert told us that he had recently held an estate sale and sold most of his possessions at the time since he was moving.

But, he said, he could not bring himself to sell this sport jacket. He just could not let it go.

OK, this now seemed to make sense. Robert had the brass buttons in a past life, and the attraction carried over to this life. But there was more. Much more.

Robert went on to tell us (the visiting entity and me) just how he acquired the brass buttons *this* time. Brass buttons that he had his tailor put on his custom cashmere sport jacket. This was not something I expected.

It seems that Robert purchased the brass buttons at an antique auction for a considerable sum. These were antique brass buttons from the US Revolutionary War era. These buttons were not just *some* brass buttons that he added to his custom made sport jacket, they were *the* actual buttons that he originally owned in his past life during the American Revolutionary War! One other thing, he mentioned that with the brass buttons at the auction was a ring. He wanted the ring, but could not afford to purchase it as part of the set that was being offered. So he only purchased the brass buttons.

I thought that this was very interesting and certainly explained the line of discussion for this session. However, there was more. Much more.

The visiting entity went on to tell Robert that during his Revolutionary War lifetime, he had one leg that was shorter than the other, which caused him to walk with a limp. The entity went on to explain that during that time period, this could be a significant disadvantage for a businessman, since any physical infirmity during that time period was often at best ridiculed and at worst could actually be fatal.

So, as the entity went on to explain, Robert in that lifetime essentially invented and constructed a special shoe. A special shoe with a lift in it to allow him to walk without a noticeable limp.

Again I wondered where this was going. I did not have to wait for long to find out.

Robert once again got up to leave the session. I sat amazed but wondered what he would return with this time.

After a few moments, Robert returned with what looked to me like a wooden shoe stretcher of some kind. Robert explained that in this life, one of his legs is shorter than the other causing him to walk with a limp. As a young adult, he had this custom shoe insert made that now allows him to walk with almost no noticeable limp at all.

### Example Number Two
### (A True Story)

Although you may have thought that Robert's three sessions per month were a lot, actually some clients have two, three, or four sessions every week, especially by phone, and especially if they are professionals in the psychology, medical, intuitive, and healing fields, or, business executives.

In this next case, the client was one of our Research Investment Partners, and he had three or four in-person sessions per week, every week, for a number of years. Our projects generally focused on metaphysical information, and the nature of consciousness, but primarily with ongoing and progressive conversations with a specific individual that the client knew personally who was now on the other side. In other words, completely different than Robert's regular sessions.

After a few years of two or three weekly research project sessions, this client asked a question about time from the perspective of a nonphysical entity. VERONICA could very well have just given her perspective and then moved on to the next subject. However, in this case, VERONICA chose to extend an invitation to other very highly evolved entities who have a specialty and interest in science, particularly mathematics and physics, to talk with us.

Note that both VERONICA and April are not particularly interested in discussing science, and April hates math.

The result of VERONICA's invitation was that some entities, including some Source Entities, as well as some historically well-known mathematicians and scientists came through over a number of sessions to discuss a now expanded topic that went well beyond just the topic of time.

One of the things that happened had never happened before. A Source Entity came through that had never before spoken to anyone physically incarnated on this planet. He stated that neither he nor any of his aspects had ever incarnated physically nor blended with any entity that had itself or had any aspects that had incarnated physically. Language to this particular entity was so primitive that he had to learn how to communicate using it. His name is Claudius.

But that was not the unusual part. This entity came through with such energy that it actually wore April out after just five or ten minutes and she had to stop. This had never happened before. As an aside that will probably get me in all kinds of trouble with the skeptics and the cynics, he did answer one question that first visit.

The client asked if he or any of the other Source Entities ever made a mistake. The Source Entity's answer was to me (science geek) interesting, to say the least.

Claudius replied most off-handedly that they had to make several adjustments to the relationship between gravity and centrifugal and centripetal force. Note again that April has no interest in science and the term centripetal force was not in her vocabulary at the time. I, of course, knew exactly what Claudius was talking about and the implications of it kind of blew my mind at the time.

But I digress.

Because Claudius was not experienced with reducing his energy level to allow him to speak without exhausting a human trance channel (April), VERONICA, behind the scenes, arranged for another who had incarnated physically and who had knowledge of science to act as a bridge. In other words, this new being would relay what Claudius had to say to us without wearing out April in the process. Again, I wish to stress that April had *never* been knocked out of a trance channeling session before. April routinely channels for several hours at a time and does not get knocked out of the sessions by phones ringing, dogs barking, talking among the group, even coughing or sneezing.

At the end of this session, before April returned, someone new picked up a pen and wrote a note on a paper that was on the coffee table before us.

It was a math formula and a name that I had never seen or heard of before. I copied it down in my notes since the original was left with the client. I soon forgot about it, since we often have many visitors of all kinds in these research sessions, and because we had so much else going on in this field at the time.

Fast forward a few months.

I find that I have made a mistake on the channel selector for my DVR. I am in a channel range that I never look at. But low and behold, I see a public television special involving the well known best selling author, Wayne Dyer.

So I tune in. Wayne Dyer is talking about consciousness in one of his presentations recorded in front of a live audience. I really respect Wayne Dyer and so I abandon my other program intentions to listen in to what he is saying.

Wayne is talking about a scientist that he admires. In fact he refers to him as one of the most influential scientists on the subject of melding science with the understanding of consciousness and spiritual metaphysics.

He mentions the name. I have never heard of this scientist. But there is something familiar about the name nonetheless.

Then I remember. I rush to get my notes from our Research Partner Investment Program session. There it is.

The name that the being gave us with the formula, that he referred to at the time as his "calling card", was the same as the name that Wayne Dyer just mentioned!

I am not certain about the formula because I cannot read my own handwritten notes. The symbol between the "F " and the "H" may be incorrect.

The formula was:

$$E = F * H$$

The name that this being wrote under the formula that he said was his calling card:

Max Planck

Fast forward a few more weeks. I did eventually talk one-on-one with Max. It was not as rewarding as I had anticipated. It seems that Max is *very* formal. He only wanted to speak German when almost every other "visitor" is willing to speak English or learn to speak English (which they can quickly do if they want to). Max also did not appreciate my sense of humor. I also got in trouble when I referred to him as "Heir Max". He immediately and sternly corrected me by saying, "No! Heir <u>Planck</u>!"

Then I also got in trouble by trying to speak a little German. When I said jokingly "Hiel", Max freaked out. It seems he had a not entirely one sided relationship with the Third Reich.

Now, if Max was the only one I got to talk with in these deep channeling sessions, it would have been worth it to me to learn German and dedicate my life to the communications.

However, given that April is an open channel, I routinely speak with many entities, and many types of entities. Four have requested a place in the writing queue for the next four books. Three of them have already started writing. Three of the four books are completely different than anything written before by anyone. The fourth book is the second part of a multi-part series being written by Source Entities.

So, we are rather busy with multiple and various projects. Accordingly, future conversations with Max will have to wait until I either learn German, or, until one of our research investment partners want to specifically focus on communicating with him.

One other thing. Many, if not most, currently "living" people today that I have heard now pronounce Max's last name as a single syllable word "Plank", as in walking the plank on a pirate ship.

However, when talking with me, Max pronounced his name with two differences:

Max pronounced his name with the "a" in Planck pronounced as a soft "o", as in "Plonk". Furthermore, he added a slight but distinct second syllable to the end of his name in the form of a soft "a". He pronounced his name when talking with me as "Plonk-a", not "Plank".

The underlying point of the above two true stories (and there are many more of them) is that evidence of life after death, and evidence of reincarnation pop up in our sessions all the time. But as far as "proof", the skeptics will likely think that I am just making it all up, or at best am delusional.

Thus, the purpose of this book is not to provide "proof".

The purpose of this book is to provide knowledge, comfort, awareness, and connection... for those who are ready for it.

-Allen, Facilitator For April Crawford

PS:  If you have an interest in life after death and/or conscious and the nature of reality specifically, the book *Seth Speaks* written by the Entity Seth via trance channel Jane Roberts is excellent and a classic.  Seth's other books are also *all* worth reading, especially *The Nature of Personal Reality* and *The Nature of the Psyche.*

If you are interested in learning to channel yourself, Sanaya Roman's classic book *Opening To Channel* will be helpful.  All of Sanaya Roman's books are good, but her book *Creating Money* is exceptional if you are interested in manifesting.

On the subject of manifesting, all of the Entity Abraham's books as written via Esther Hicks are good on this subject.  Abraham is the Entity that recently has really helped promote the saying "The Law of Attraction".  This universal law is what the Entity Seth termed "Like Attracts Like".

If you have a general interest in spiritual metaphysic and the nature of consciousness, also check out these authors:

Wayne Dyer, Deepak Chopra, Robert Schwartz, John Edward, James Van Praagh, Edgar Cayce, and don't forget Oprah Winfrey, who is way more spiritually attuned than some may realize. Oprah Winfrey has also been very bold by sharing her interest in spiritual metaphysics given her media success in other areas.

# About the Author

April Crawford is an AMAZON Top 50 Best Selling Author, and is also one of the world's most naturally talented and adept Full Body Open Deep Trance Channels.

April has clients in most countries of the world, who mostly consult with the highly evolved entity and guide known as VERONICA about relationships, business, life coaching, and spiritual and personal related growth issues.

April's spiritual newsletter, *"Inner Whispers"*, is written mostly by the entity VERONICA, and is read by tens of thousands of readers each week.    It is available (free) at: www.InnerWhispers.net

April currently lives in Los Angeles, California with her husband, Allen, and her many pets.

***

## OTHER BOOKS
## BY
## APRIL CRAWFORD

*Dear VERONICA*
*Letters To And From A Spirit Guide*
Available also as a Kindle Book
www.DearVERONICA.net


*"Inner Whispers":*
*Messages From A Spirit Guide (Volume I)*
Available also as a Kindle Book
www.InnerWhispersTheBook.com


*"Inner Whispers":*
*Messages From A Spirit Guide (Volume II)*
Available also as a Kindle Book
www.InnerWhispersTheBook.com


*"Parting Notes": A Connection With The Afterlife*
Also available as a Kindle Book
www.PartingNotes.com

**Ashram Tang... a Story... and a Discovery**

Also available as a Kindle Book.

www.AshramTang.com

**Reflections of a Spiritual Astronaut: Book I**

Available as a Kindle Book.

**Reflections of a Spiritual Astronaut: Book II**

Available as a Kindle Book.

**your life and its choices: THE RECIPE FOR ASCENTION TO ANOTHER PLANE "A" TO "Z"**

By Ish and Osco (Spirit Guides) via April Crawford

Available as a Kindle Book.

**Deep Trance Channeling Sessions:**
**Special Edition No.1**

Available as a Kindle Book

For more information about the Author or about True Open Deep Trance Channeling: www.AprilCrawford.com

For the free spiritual newsletter *"Inner Whispers"*
www.InnerWhispers.net.

For personal telephone or in-person consultations via
April Crawford, Personal Appearances, or Media
Interviews, contact Allen at AprilReadings@aol.com

\*\*\*